ENDURING
MINISTRY

WISDOM FROM
VETERAN PASTORS FOR
MANAGING STRESS &
AVOIDING BURNOUT

JACKSON ANDREW HESTER, PhD

Foreword by Josh Taylor

© 2022 Areopagus Publishing: Mobile, AL

ISBN: 978-1-66782-113-9
eBook ISBN: 978-1-66782-864-0

FOREWORD

I worked hard. Every day. And Jack almost fired me because of it.

Many of us have worked for bosses that would have preferred us to spend more time at work, not less. We've had those bosses that call us on the weekends, reward us for never taking a day off, and praise us for being the first one in and the last one to leave.

I was the kind of person that boss would have loved. I loved what I did. I loved ministry. I was good at it. There was nowhere I'd rather be than in my office organizing an event or creating the perfect system to keep up with our new guests, members, and giving.

My co-ministers were my best friends. Our office was fun, comfortable, and productive.

When you work as a pastor under Jack Hester's leadership, you get a lot of freedom. Jack's not a micromanager. Instead, he works hard to build his team with people he doesn't have to micromanage.

You see, the beauty of working for someone that doesn't have a giant ego is that he's not afraid to surround himself with people that are better at things than he is.

I was given the freedom to create. I was given the freedom to try new things. And I was given the freedom to fail.

However, I found out one day, there was something I didn't have the freedom to do. Overwork.

About 5 years into my time working at Mars Hill Church in Mobile, AL, I was becoming tired, teetering on burnout, and my fuse was getting a little short.

My wife made comments about the time I was spending at the office and how much she would love it if I were home for dinner more, wasn't scooting out every Saturday morning to get last minute things done at the office, and didn't spend the entire Sunday at the church.

Jack wasn't monitoring my time. But one thing he always made clear was, your ministry is to your family first.

At the time, my wife and I had no children. We were young, in our late 20's with little responsibility. I didn't think it was a big deal to spend more time at the office. In fact, I figured my wife loved the extra time to herself after work.

But the overwork quickly began to change me. Not only did it start to become my identity, but it also started to become my purpose. I wasn't good at delegation. I wasn't good at giving credit to others. And I wasn't good at taking a break.

The excuse for my overwork was that the church deserved it. It was my calling. My ministry. This is Jesus' bride and I should be giving her my all. That was a giant cop-out.

The reality was, it was me. It was my pride. My selfishness. My throne.

One day Jack walked into my office to check on me. He was noticing the change in me. I assumed he was walking into my office to praise me for one of the amazing ideas I executed.

Quite the opposite. Jack gently and humbly thanked me for the work I was doing. He appreciated the commitment I had to the church and for my strong work ethic.

Then he said, "We have a problem. You're not taking your day off."

You see, everyone was expected to take Saturday off and one day during the week off. These were days to be spent with family, not at work.

Our day during the week was meant for Sabbath. Refresh. The day I chose was Friday.

But I never took Friday off. Instead, I worked on Fridays. Every Friday. There was always more to do. More to plan. More to fix.

"Our church is only as healthy as our leaders", Jack said. "Part of being healthy is taking time to rest, pray, and enjoy being with Jesus. If you're not taking your day off and you're in the office 50-60 hours per week, I have to assume you're not doing much resting."

I pushed back. "Work is my rest. I can't relax knowing there are things that need to be done. It's all I would be able to think about."

"And that's the problem. If it's all you'd be able to think about, then it's consuming you. There are always going to be things that need to be done. There are always going to be people that need you. But you're not giving them your best if you're not becoming your best.

I'm going to go ahead and let you know, because I care about you, your family, and our church: If you don't start taking your weekday off immediately, along with Saturdays, I'm going to have to fire you."

That day changed my life.

I wish I could say it was a 180 turn for me. It took time. It took time to change my mindset. It took time to change my motivation. It took time to change my heart.

Today, I make controlling my time a priority. I keep a tight schedule and make sure I always block time off for rest, my family, and leisure.

I still work hard. I still love what I do. But I've learned to listen to my mind and my body. I've learned to give myself margin so I can say 'yes' to my family more.

I've learned to sit at the feet of Jesus and listen often.

My story may have turned out very different if Jack had never had the wisdom to fire me if I didn't stop the overwork and learn to truly rest.

Jack has been teaching me the contents of this book for almost two decades. His research, stories, and advice will change your ministry; you'll see new opportunities to make an impact in your life and in the lives of others around you.

Josh Taylor

DEDICATION:

This book is dedicated to all of my fellow co-laborers in the ministry of Jesus Christ... May you find encouragement in these pages, may you sense many partners in suffering and may you find a renewal in your relationship with God.

ACKNOWLEDGEMENTS:

I want to thank my wife Brandi and my three kids Collin, Caleb, and Caroline for the time and energy that they allowed me to sacrifice to make this project possible. They inspire me in so many ways that it would be impossible to mention them all.

My mom and dad, for all the years they invested in me and encouraged me to "press on." I wish my mom could have lived to see the finished product of this project.

Drs. Michael Wilder, Hal Pettegrew, and Shane Parker for the influence and mentorship they provided me throughout the years.

To the staff and people of Mars Hill Church in Mobile and Fairhope, Alabama as well as those at Harbor Community Church. A true forever family that allowed me to fail and also celebrated successes with me in true family fashion.

Lastly, but not least, thanks to Len Woods for his direction, insight, and expertise in the editing process of this book… invaluable!

This project would have never made it this far without the contribution and influence of all these friends and family… Thank you!

CONTENTS

INTRODUCTION:
Why Are So Many Pastors Running on Empty?

MEET DAMIAN...

It's 8 a.m. on Sunday. In the dilapidated building that once was a cafeteria, a tall African-American man is quickly putting folding chairs in rows. Meet Damian, the 29-year-old pastor of City Church, a small but growing church plant in L.A.

The two guys who volunteered to set up didn't show up. So now Damian is doing that job . . . while trying to go over his sermon in his head . . . *and* texting back and forth with his wife Shondra.

Shondra is not a happy camper this morning. She's reporting that their boys (ages 5 and 3) are "being little you-know-whats" and that she won't be at church because she doesn't want "to inflict their misbehavior on the whole church."

Damian gently downplays it all. He writes, "Aw baby they're just being boys." But deep down, he knows the truth. Shondra looks for reasons to disengage. She hasn't been on board with this whole "church planting thing" since the very beginning.

Some backstory: Fourteen months ago, Damian—who *can* be impulsive at times—abruptly left his high-paying sales job to follow what he insists was "the clear call of God." Since then, Damian and Shondra have burned through their savings, because he's only taking home about 40% of what he was making in sales. Clearly, his young church hasn't yet gotten the hang of giving. This means things at Damian's house are as tight financially as they are tense relationally.

Don't get the wrong idea. Damian's not irresponsible. And he's not a jerk of a husband. If you met him, you'd love him. He's a born leader. When this big 6'5" ex-defensive end walks into a room, he commands attention. Un-churched, irreligious people are drawn to him. Probably because it's obvious he loves and accepts everybody just the way they are.

Damian's funny, outgoing, and *real*—he came to faith in his early twenties after a pretty wild life. No wonder his young church already has 150-175 people showing up most Sundays.

Despite the long hours and meager pay, Damian loves what he's doing—even the crazy and chaotic days. He's driven to see City Church become a powerful force for God in the community. Though he has no formal training, he loves preaching. To get better he's taking some Bible classes online.

Ask Damian what would help him, and he'd tell you "better organizational skills, more sleep, and an assistant (not necessarily in that order)."

Ask Shondra and she'd tell you Damian desperately needs a HUGE pay bump, the ability to say "no," and an assistant (because right now, he's pretty much a one-man show).

* * * * *

MEET PASTOR KEN...

At 1:30 on a sunny Wednesday afternoon Pastor Ken, 45, is sermon prepping or trying to. But no matter how hard he tries, he *cannot* keep his eyes open.

This is because he woke up—again—at 3:30 a.m. When his eyes fluttered open, his mind went from 0-60 mph in about four seconds.

Instantly he was overwhelmed by dark, troubling thoughts. Here's a quick list of some of the uncomfortable questions that gathered in Ken's head like a thunderstorm:

- *A year ago we had 425 members. Now we're at 390. God, why are people leaving? What am I doing wrong?*

- *What am I supposed to do about this growing "worship song controversy"?*

- *And, God forbid, what if the Lambrights leave over that?*

  [Reader's note: Seven or eight months back the congregation started singing some songs from Hillsong and Bethel Music. The younger families in the church have enthusiastically embraced these contemporary worship choruses. But some of the older members of the congregation are unhappy with certain lyrics (as well as the theology of the songwriters).

  Robert Lambright happens to be in this older group. He's a church board member, the outspoken CEO of a successful tech company— and he and his wife are the biggest contributors to the church. How big? Let's just say that each year they give an amount equal to about a *quarter* of the annual budget.]

- *Should I confront Ryan—again—today?*

  [Reader's note: Ryan is the popular youth pastor at St. Andrews Presbyterian. His carefree, laid-back style clashes with Ken's intense, deliberate, organized personality. Ken thinks Ryan is passive-aggressive, sometimes openly insubordinate. He also thinks his teaching is superficial. He'd like it to be deeper. (Actually, what he'd *really* like, is to go back in time and never hire Ryan in the first place.)]

- *God, why do you seem so distant? I'm seeking you, but I can't seem to find you. Where are you?*

[Readers note: To complicate matters, Ken has been struggling spiritually for a while. Ever experience the "Dark Night of the Soul"? That's where Ken finds himself. Despite faithfully engaging in spiritual practices, Ken has no sense of God's presence in his life. It's been this way for months. His prayers feel lifeless. *He* feels lifeless.

This is the cyclone of thoughts that whirled in Pastor Ken's brain for at least 30 minutes as he lay there in the dark. Finally, he gave up and got out of bed quietly. He read his Bible, showered, and dressed. By 5:30 he was in the McDonald's drive-thru. At 6 a.m. he was in his office at his desk.

So now at 1:30 p.m., it's no wonder he's sleepy! He picks up the phone, buzzes his assistant, and says, "I'll be back in 30 minutes."

Pastor Ken exits the building the back way (to avoid seeing anyone in the front office). He gets in his car and gets on the interstate. He's going one exit west to the Starbucks on Thomas Road.

But as he nears his exit, he thinks *What if I just kept driving? What if I didn't stop till I got to the Grand Canyon? I want to go off the grid. For two months. Maybe three. I should just be like Ryan…do whatever the heck I feel like doing! I've been at St. Andrews 10 years. If those elders won't give me a sabbatical, I should just go ahead and take it!*

Ken comes back to reality; he can't go AWOL. He dutifully exits, and as he does, he notices a landscape crew sprucing up the grounds of a fancy law firm. For a moment he actually feels envious of them. *All they do is cut grass all day. No people hassles. No worship wars. Just mindless mowing.*

As he sits in the Starbucks drive-thru, he looks across the way at two guys with weed whackers. *Wonder what those guys make? Could I feed my family doing yard work?*

* * * * *

MEET BROTHER CHARLES

At 10:57 on a rainy Thursday night, Brother Charles sets his alarm and slumps heavily into bed.

He's the senior pastor of Christ Community Church, a big, independent church (with Baptist roots) in the Birmingham suburbs. Charles is extroverted and playful—some would even say, "charming." He's typically high-energy and optimistic. Tonight, not so much.

Most nights Charles *passes out* inside of 90 seconds. Tonight, he's still awake at 11:30. He can't stop replaying the events of his crazy day.

It started with fireworks in an early morning board meeting. Two strong-willed elders (who have been going at each other since before Charles got to Christ Community 14 years ago) got into a heated argument. At issue? Whether a female missionary should be allowed to speak in the Sunday morning service. For 30+ minutes Pete and Byron tossed Bible verses at each other like hand grenades, debating the difference between "sharing" and "preaching"

This contentious meeting was followed by a walk-in visit from a weeping member of the congregation who's freshly widowed. After an hour of counseling (mostly sitting quietly, listening, nodding, and handing her tissues), Brother Charles answered emails for 45 minutes (dealing with 17 of the 41 already in his box).

Then he switched gears, embarking on some sermon prep, pausing multiple times to wonder things like: *Why in God's good name did I decide to preach through the Book of Hebrews? How is it already Thursday? Does every pastor of a 2,000 member, multi-campus church feel like he's being dragged around by the ankles?*

At 11:30 a.m. the 53-year-old pastor grabbed his Bible and hustled down to the Commons to do a little Q & A with the Thursday Ladies' Bible Study. (They're going through the Book of Nehemiah—and Brother Charles, everyone knows, did his dissertation on Nehemiah.)

This lunchtime interaction consisted of some amazing food, three questions about Nehemiah, followed by a barrage of very pointed questions about the new guitarist on the worship team—a tall, skinny college kid—who had *not* removed his baseball cap during worship on Sunday. It was half an hour of corporate lament, peppered with statements like "what's wrong with young people these days anyways?"

From 1:20-1:45, Charles was on the phone trying to soothe Pete, one of the worked-up elders from the morning skirmish. After that, he grabbed another cup of coffee (his fourth of the day).

When he checked his email again and found 57 unopened messages in his box, he shut his computer.

At 2 p.m. Brother Charles and his executive pastor Bryan were on a Zoom call interviewing another applicant for the church's open youth minister position. (This was candidate number *nine*, and five minutes in, Charles knew there would be a tenth.)

At 3, just as he was sitting down to do some more sermon prep, Charles got a frantic call from his wife that there was water in the basement . . . water that smelled like sewage. The second he set his phone down, he got an even more frantic call from Mr. Grafton that Mrs. Grafton had been taken to the hospital with what EMTs feared was a stroke. Brother Charles spent the next two hours sitting with Mr. Grafton in the ER. He then rushed home to gulp down dinner, inspect the basement, and head out to the men's group he leads every Thursday night.

Now, staring at the ceiling, Brother Charles groans audibly as he remembers what's on his schedule for Friday—mostly his unfinished sermon out of Hebrews 6.

"What's wrong?" his groggy wife asks.

"Aw, nothing. It can wait till tomorrow," he replies.

Wouldn't you know it is "tomorrow" before Brother Charles finally dozes off.

* * * * *

Any of that sound familiar? Any of those scenarios hit home for you? Have you ever felt like Damian…or Pastor Ken…or Brother Charles? Maybe as you read this sentence you feel some of what they're feeling?

If so, you're in the right book!

THE GOAL OF THIS BOOK

Even though I don't know you, I bet I can make a pretty good guess about you . . . and about your mission in life.

**You want to be a healthy pastor who pleases God and
makes an eternal difference in the lives of others.**

(How'd I do?)

I'm sure you'd say it differently. But in so many words, I bet that's what you want. If so, that's a good, God-honoring goal. To see that happen you're going to need both the wisdom and the tools necessary for going the distance in ministry.

The problem—as seen in the lives of the three pastors you just met—is this: Pastoral leadership brings ministers face-to-face with all sorts of stressors. And those daily pressures and assorted trials can eventually wear you down and make you feel like quitting.

Call me crazy, but I don't think God meant for ministry to be a beat down. And I sure don't believe it has to end in burnout. I believe there's a better way.

As a pastor for 30 years, I know how difficult and draining it is to lead a church and care for people's souls. That's why when it was time to do my own doctoral dissertation, I decided to focus on pastoral stress and burnout. I interviewed 20 long-term pastors of assorted churches. I asked them "How'd you do it? How'd you manage to endure the hardest times of ministry and yet keep fighting the good fight of faith? How'd you avoid burning out? What have you learned that you can pass on?" Their sage answers, my own experiences, and the insights of other pastors I know form the bulk of this book.

I'm convinced the collective wisdom in these pages can help you thrive—not just survive—in ministry. But that can only happen if you'll do three things:

1. **Read** these short chapters (preferably with another pastor friend or two).

2. **Reflect** on and process the content (again, by batting around the provided questions with one or two others).

3. **Respond** by actually following the counsel of these older, wiser pastors. Pick one thing from each chapter and *do it*.

If you'll follow this simple plan, I believe with all my heart, you can avoid stressing out and burning out. Instead, you'll have more peace and joy in ministry, and you'll become the kind of pastor people want to follow.

Please, if you're a newbie in ministry, pay attention. The counsel here can save you a *lot* of grief. And if you've been a pastor for a while, but you're at your wit's end and maybe even thinking about throwing in the towel, I urge you to take the time to digest what's in these pages. This book will remind you of some crucial truths. It will give you some practical tools. It will, I pray, help you recapture your love for God and people.

THE NEED FOR THIS BOOK

I don't want to be redundant. But I'm about to be redundant. (That's how strongly I feel about this topic.)

This is serious stuff. Statistics tell us that one out of every three pastors will burn out within the first five years of ministry.[1] That's both frightening and tragic. The old quip—"Ninety percent of all pastors consider leaving the ministry at some point in their career. And the other 10 percent are liars."—is almost certainly true.

And yet there is hope. Not *every* pastor succumbs to the pressure, then crashes and burns. Some are able to thrive even in the middle of stress-filled ministries. Their lives and ministries aren't problem-free because there's no such thing in a fallen, broken world.

Yet these wise souls show us that burnout is *not* inevitable. It's not written in stone that every pastor has to succumb to stress. We *can* do something about this stress/burnout problem.

I'll say it again. This book grew out of the interviews I did with pastors who have demonstrated resilience in the face of the stressful minefield of ministry. They didn't quit.

To the rich wisdom of those men, I've also added the insights of other pastors I know, plus some lessons from my own experience. The result for you—I hope—will be like sitting with a bunch of flawed but good-hearted servants of God. It's a chance to absorb hundreds of years of pastoral experience from men who've seen what works and what doesn't.

Friend, within these pages are all the themes and insights that emerged from my conversations. I share all of it with you, one pastor to another, in the hope that you will learn from those who've gone before you. I want to see you thrive wherever you find yourself.

Bottom line: If you're engaging in habits that have you headed for trouble, I am going to try to get you to re-think your direction. If you're drowning in the waves of discouragement, I want to see you get the help you desperately need. Whatever your current state, the goal is to equip you to get a better handle on stress, before it manhandles you.

LOOKING FORWARD

Most people like to know, "Where are we going?" so here's the plan . . .

In the first half of this book, we'll look more closely at the *problem* of pastoral stress and the grim reality of burnout. What are the issues that are knocking so many pastors out of commission?

In the latter half of this book, we'll get immensely practical and discuss how you can create a realistic *plan* for coping with stress and avoiding burnout.

The problem and the plan. That's as simple as I can make it.

At the end of the book, you'll find a couple of practical tools for helping you (a) assess how you're doing; and (b) remember the truths that can anchor your soul.

Sound good?

If so, let's get going.

THE **PROBLEM** OF PASTORAL STRESS & BURNOUT

CHAPTER 1

All Stressed Up and Nowhere (Good) to Go

After getting a peek into:

- Damian's chaotic church plant

- Pastor Ken's restless congregation and dry, exhausted soul

- Brother Charles' overwhelming "megachurch" responsibilities . . . What else can we say but . . .

*Ministry is **hard**.*

This truth shouldn't surprise any of us. Not if we've read the gospels. Have we forgotten how the apostle Paul famously described *his* life in ministry:

"Five times I received from the Jews the forty lashes minus one. Three times I was beaten with rods, once I was pelted with stones, three times I was shipwrecked, I spent a night and a day in the open sea, I have been constantly on the move. I have been in danger from rivers, in danger from bandits, in danger from my fellow Jews, in danger from Gentiles; in danger in the city, in danger in the country, in danger at sea; and in danger from false believers. I have labored and toiled and have often

gone without sleep; I have known hunger and thirst and have often gone without food; I have been cold and naked. Besides everything else, I face daily the pressure of my concern for all the churches."
(2 Corinthians 11:24–28, NIV)

Thankfully, most of us don't have the pressures and problems Paul faced. (Have you gone without food this week? Been shipwrecked lately?)

And yet, we definitely have our share of modern stressors.

I have been a pastor in the same church for almost 20 years now. I've faced incredible struggles and had days when I wanted to do ANYTHING but be a pastor.

I vividly remember one Sunday morning hiding in one of the closets in the kid's area because I heard voices calling my name! Our church was growing and so were the demands on me and even my family I felt neither ready nor worthy for the challenges that were coming my way.

It was in that closet that God whispered some words to my heart. As I sat there, wanting to be ANYWHERE else, I received the encouragement and perspective that my soul needed: "Go on out there. I got this. Just stay out my way and everything will be fine."

Those words became my answer to everything… "Jack, how are we going to handle this crisis?" I'd respond, "We are going to stay out of God's way." Someone would ask, "How did you grow this church into what it is today?" My standard response was, "I just tried to stay out of God's way."

In short, I am a fellow pilgrim with you. Needless to say, I have not arrived. I am still on the journey too. We're in these things together.

As we begin, we should probably define terms. We keep using the word *stress*.

WHAT EXACTLY IS STRESS?

Stress can be defined as the tension we feel when facing pressure (of any kind). It's the burden we experience mentally, physically, emotionally, and spiritually when we're carrying a heavy load.

Check a thesaurus for synonyms for "stress" and you'll find words like *anxiety, tension, trauma, hassle,* and *worry.* (And all the ministers shouted, "Amen!")

Someone has quipped: "Cram together the *strain* of tough situations with all the *pressures* people and events put on us and the result is *stress.*"

Makes sense to me: **STR**ain + pr**ESS**ures = **STRESS**

But how does it show up in the lives of pastors? I believe ministerial stress is the cumulative weight of trying to . . .

- Accomplish goals
- Meet expectations
- Fulfill duties

. . . even as you:

- Face opposition
- Overcome obstacles
- Solve messy problems

In other words, we're trying to do good and godly things; but an array of forces and pressures continually come against us to complicate our efforts. No wonder we're tired!

Stress is real. It isn't just a modern word used by weak people to whine about their lives. And it's more, way more, than a mere feeling. It's actually physical. When money is tight . . . when people start leaving the church . . . when two of your elders get into a verbal brawl right before your eyes . . . your body literally goes on high alert. Here's how doctors describe it:

> "When you feel threatened, a chemical reaction occurs in your body that allows you to act in a way to prevent injury. This reaction is known as 'fight-or-flight,' or the stress response. *During a stress response, your heart rate increases, breathing quickens, muscles tighten, and blood pressure rises.* You've gotten ready to act. It is how you protect yourself."[1]

That powerful chemical your body releases—adrenalin—is exactly what you need for sudden, short-term emergencies. This stress response is a self-protection mechanism. But when you *stay* in a stressed-out, high alert state for long periods—running all day every day on adrenalin—it's only a matter of time until you crash. Your body can't keep that up. Neither can your soul.

THE KINDS OF STRESSORS

We don't need the stories of Damian, Pastor Ken, and Brother Charles to tell us that stress can be generated by lots of different things. But their situations are a good reminder. Stressors come at us constantly from every direction.

Ever see or complete the Holmes-Rahe Life Stress Inventory? It's a checklist (you can find it online) that assigns a "stress number" to 43 common life events.

So, for example, Holmes and Rahe say a divorce generates about 73 stress points, being fired counts for 47, an outstanding personal achievement comes to 28 (yes, even good things can be stressful), and a change in sleep habits measures 16 points.

---

1   https://www.webmd.com/balance/stress-management/
    stress-symptoms-effects_of-stress-on-the-body

Most people take issue with the points assigned in the Holmes-Rahe scale. They argue that the points awarded to the various events are off—too high in some cases, too low in others. Perhaps. But that misses the point of the inventory.

The idea is to read through the list, see how many tumultuous events you've experienced over the previous year, and take stock. As far as the test makers are concerned, if you've accumulated fewer than 150 points, you are considered low risk for any sort of stress-induced health breakdown. But heaven help you if you've racked up more than 300 points. You need relief, and quickly!

Later in this book, we'll show a similar "stress" inventory for pastors (minus the points).

For now, let's just point out that stress is quite varied. It can be both:

- **Chronic** and **Acute**. *Chronic* stressors are low-grade. They're not loud and dramatic, just persistent. They nag you. They poke at you. For a church plant like Damian's that doesn't yet have a home, "Where are we meeting?" will be a chronic stress, at least until they find a facility. (Then they'll have chronic stress about something else—like the HVAC system that keeps going out.) For a lot of pastors, preaching is a chronic stress (because Sunday has this funny way of rolling around *every single week*).

  Acute stressors are different. They're sudden. They come out of left field unexpectedly, screaming for attention. They don't poke you in an irritating way; they punch you in the face! An acute stress could be anything from your facility being vandalized, to a key staff member abruptly quitting.

- **Short-term** and **Long-term**. *Short-term* stressors last only for a season. Your associate is taking a much-deserved sabbatical this summer and you have to pick up some of his duties. It'll be extra work, but at least it's only till mid-August.

Long-term stressors unpack their bags and stick around. They're the pressures we face constantly because we live in a fallen world. You will always have a few critical church members. That's not going to change until Jesus comes back. (And some of those grumblers will likely complain even then about the Lord's timing!)

- **Avoidable** and **unavoidable**. *Avoidable* stressors are unnecessary pressures we bring on ourselves. Like the staff member who continually causes drama. News flash—he *could* be let go. Or like the pastor who is frantic every Saturday night (or every Sunday morning before sunrise!) trying to pull a sermon together at the last minute. It doesn't have to be this way. That pastor *could* change his schedule and enjoy peaceful Saturday nights and Sunday mornings.

  Unavoidable stressors are all the things over which we have no control: beloved church members dying. Valuable leaders getting transferred and moving. Pandemics putting your people out of work. There's nothing to do in such cases but trust God.

- **Positive** and **Negative**. We know all about *negative* stress. But *positive* stress? Is that a typo? No. Some stress *is* actually beneficial. It was endocrinologist Hans Selye who affixed the Greek prefix eu- (meaning "good") to the word stress, to coin the word *eustress*, literally "good stress." Eustress is psychologically healthy stress.

  Think of the pressure that motivates you to jump out of the way of an approaching car. Or the pressure you feel to go to work (so you can get a paycheck) or go work out (so you can battle that bulging waistline). The fact is some stress in life *is* beneficial.

  Ministers in one study claimed that a certain degree of stress was energizing and, in fact, essential for optimal daily functioning.

Stress didn't keep them from doing what they were made to do. On the contrary, it fueled them.[2]

WHY IS STRESS SUCH A BIG DEAL?

That's such an important question, let's save it for the next chapter.

For now, let's pause and consider some . . .

QUESTIONS FOR REFLECTION AND DISCUSSION

- Which of the three pastors in the introduction do you relate to most and why?

- If you could give a brief word of counsel to any of those guys, what would it be?

- How would you define *stress* to a first-grader?

- What are the three biggest stressors in your life right now and what kinds of stressors are they?

- What thought from either the introduction or this chapter hit you the hardest? Why?

CHAPTER 2

Why Stress Is a Big, Bad Deal

I'm guessing that if Damian and Brother Charles were to sit down and take the Holmes-Rahe Stress Inventory, they'd score pretty high. And Pastor Ken? His stress point tally might be in the stratosphere!

Poor Ken. He's facing so many heavy pressures. Families are leaving. Influential members are disgruntled. He's got a popular staff member he wishes he hadn't hired. His long-term spiritual dryness has left him bewildered and blah.

Things at home are fine. That's a bright spot. Except for the fact that his kids are teenagers. Ken knows he's going to blink a few times, and—poof!—they'll be out of the nest. He feels extra pressure to make the most of the time they have left.

Add it all up. That's a *lot* to carry around.

It doesn't help matters that Ken has workaholic tendencies. Or that he's a perfectionist. Or that his diet is pretty terrible, he has no regular exercise regimen, no hobbies to replenish him, no deep friendships nearby. Are we really surprised stress has him near the breaking point?

In "normal" times, Ken is quiet, serious, and introverted. Lately, he's subdued and withdrawn to the point of being grim.

Thankfully, he and his wife have a two-day getaway coming up. (What a shame it can't be a three-month sabbatical!)

Ken's plight raises urgent questions, among them:

*How many ministers are stressed out like he is
and barely hanging on by a thread?
Where does such heavy stress lead if it's not addressed?*

STRESS AND THE GROWING PROBLEM OF PASTORAL BURNOUT

The term *burnout* was first used in the 1970s to describe those in the helping professions who were:

- Feeling drained and exhausted on an ongoing basis

- Suffering a loss of commitment and motivation; and

- Developing cynical attitudes.

Psychologists started experiencing these symptoms when working with clients at an alternative health care center.[3]

Hence, the first serious studies of burnout grew out of the work of caring, helping, and healing professionals – professionals whose work depends upon *interpersonal interactions*. And that's a pretty good snapshot of what burnout is: feeling drained, exhausted, unmotivated, apathetic, and cynical.

Pastoral burnout is now such a widespread problem that some call it an *epidemic*. Part of the problem may be due to the unique role of pastors in the modern world. It seems like the expectations (and job descriptions) grow every day.

In many churches, besides being a model husband and devoted dad, the pastor is expected to be a scintillating preacher, a people magnet, a wise counselor, a respected leader in the community, a competent staff director, *and* a cultural expert. On any given day, a pastor can also find himself handling IT problems, overseeing the "business" of the church, doing custodial work, dealing with HR issues, solving church "marketing" problems, feeling pressured to have some kind of social media presence, and engaging in conflict management!

In light of all these expectations and responsibilities (and that's *not* even a complete list!), pastors are dropping like flies. And, honestly, who can blame them?

The stats and stories about burnout are beyond shocking. My point being: Burnout is *not* a made-up buzzword. It's real.

For many pastors, burnout usually leads to dropping out of ministry. For others, it leads to packing up and moving on to another church. The problem with taking another church, of course, is that you take your weary, worn-out soul (and whatever personal dysfunctions you've got) with you to the new church…the new church that has its own unique set of problems and pressures! Not a recipe for success!

What does all this stress do to us?

THE EFFECTS OF STRESS ON PHYSICAL HEALTH

Forty percent of the pastors I interviewed admitted having *physical ailments* associated with excessive stress.

Intestinal issues, insomnia, high blood pressure, and sexual problems were all mentioned. (I should note that experts tell us stress can both *cause* and *exacerbate* such physical conditions.)

Research has shown that other stress-related physical issues can include:

- Cardiovascular disease, abnormal heart rhythms, heart attacks, and stroke
- Obesity and eating disorders
- Skin issues like acne, eczema, and psoriasis

- Hair loss

This echoes a survey of United Methodist clergy in North Carolina that revealed alarmingly high rates of obesity, diabetes, asthma, arthritis, hypertension, and depression among the pastors studied.

Interestingly, these ministers rated their health to be better than it actually was! (Proof that we aren't always as objective as we think we are.)

On a positive note, the majority of the pastors I interviewed (seventy-five percent) reported engaging in some form of health-related stress relief. Most engaged in regular physical exercise, and two pastors insisted that getting sufficient sleep is essential for health.[4]

We'll talk more about those antidotes to stress when we get to the second half of this book.

THE EFFECTS OF STRESS ON MENTAL AND EMOTIONAL HEALTH

As the Methodist clergy study showed, unrelenting stress doesn't only create physical problems. It can also lead to mental health issues like depression (and anxiety and personality disorders).

One pastor I know admitted:

"I had the task of trying to shepherd a church through the trauma of another pastor's moral failure. This triggered a lot of 'old church baggage' in a lot of people. It was ugly—and for months and months. I got stressed to the point that I was showing all the classic signs of burnout and clinical depression—apathy, excessive sleeping, inability to think clearly, becoming reclusive. At my wife's insistence, I finally went to my doctor. He prescribed some anti-depressants. I also started seeing a counselor to get to the roots of my issues. And I started exercising more.

"Part of me felt 'weak' for getting to the place where I needed that kind of help. To be honest, I worried what others might think or say—until I remembered that some of the saints in Scripture battled depression. Bottom line, I'm glad I did all those things. Over time I *did* get better. My light-hearted, playful personality returned. I'm not on anti-depressants anymore, but there's no doubt they helped. Thank God for medicine that can level out the chemicals in your brain!"

THE EFFECTS OF STRESS AND
BURNOUT ON BEHAVIOR

Earlier, I mentioned how even *success* can be stressful. And when the success is extreme, it can take a pastor out.

We've seen this happen so many times. Big-name pastors become idolized by large congregations (or national or even international followings). These leaders soon start to believe all the hype surrounding them. Often, because of all their "success" and popularity, they become self-absorbed and proud. This invariably leads to reckless judgment in interpersonal relationships.

The research actually shows a strong correlation between high levels of stress (whether caused by success or duress) and sexual misconduct.

What follows in such cases is both tragic and predictable: these unhealthy leaders create toxic systems and cultures around them. Or they become abusive. Or they engage in unethical conduct or immoral behavior. Or all of the above. As one old pastor put it, "Dysfunctional leaders create dysfunctional systems."

A study of Southern Baptist senior pastors revealed exactly this. There were personality factors in most cases of pastoral wrongdoing. Many of these fallen leaders were found to have strong narcissistic tendencies. Many had self-esteem issues (that is, their sense of self-worth was largely dependent on external factors like admiration from others).

These kinds of issues make pastors vulnerable to impulsive and self-destructive behaviors. They often act out in response to their stress. They often don't burn out quietly. They flame out in very public ways, and many people suffer as a result.[5]

All this is why stress is a big, bad deal. When it's not acknowledged and addressed healthily, it too often leads to burnout and other outcomes nobody wants.

Stress will affect you physically, emotionally—perhaps even morally. It will take you out if you don't learn to process it.

If that's not a wake-up call, I'm not sure what is.

QUESTIONS FOR REFLECTION AND DISCUSSION

- What comes to mind when you hear the word *burnout*?

- Have you ever been a victim of burnout? What was that like?

- How would you say your current stress is affecting you right now physically? Emotionally?

- Why do you think there is such a stigma attached to depression?

- Why are so many Christians skeptical of things like therapy and antidepressants?

- If Pastor Ken were a buddy of yours, what would you encourage him to do?

- What thought from this chapter hits you the hardest? Why?

CHAPTER 3

Does Stress Have Any Upside?

As seen in the lives of Damian, Ken, and Charles—and in the comments from pastors I interviewed—stress is real. (Like you didn't know that.) Here's what we're seeing and saying,

Handled poorly, stress leads to grim, life-altering effects.

Hopefully, this little book is serving as a cautionary tale for you. I pray you're being nudged (or perhaps even elbowed hard in the heart) to take inventory of your own soul and ministry.

So, okay. Stress has a scary side. But is it all bad? All the time?

No.

As mentioned in chapter 1, there is such a thing as "beneficial stress" (termed *eustress*). This is the kind of stress that motivates and/or energizes us to accomplish necessary things. More on that shortly.

First, consider this counterintuitive truth: As followers we Christ, we're commanded to "give thanks in all circumstances" (Ephesians 5:18, NIV). Notice, the apostle Paul doesn't say to give thanks *for* all circumstances." To be thankful *for* the stress of an ugly church split? To express gratitude *for* the arsonist who set the fire that gutted your facility? That would be a weird, masochistic kind of faith.

No, Paul says we're to be thankful *in* all circumstances. Why? Probably because of another great spiritual reality he expressed: "We know that in all things God works for the good of those who love him" (Romans 8:28, NIV).

This has got to be one of the most comforting of all biblical truths: God can (and does) bring good even out of the worst and hardest things in life.

That means he can use the pressures we're facing to conform us "to the likeness of his Son" (Romans 8:29). In other words, stress, when we approach it correctly, can shape us and make us like Jesus.

I heard this idea expressed again and again in my interviews. Consider some of the "benefits" stress can bring our way:

STRESS WILL DRIVE US TO CHRIST.

The majority of the pastors I interviewed absolutely believed that stress had a *positive spiritual effect* on them. It drove them to a deeper walk with God. Listen to their testimonies:

- "To me, that's one positive about stress. It drives me to Jesus. The more stressed I am, the more time I spend in the prayer closet. You know, when the bills are paid and the dogs aren't barking in the neighborhood in the middle of the night and the deacons are happy, I'm less inclined to seek the Lord than when I'm in crisis mode. Anything that drives me to Jesus is good for me, and stress is the kind of thing that drives me closer and closer to him. It forces me to cast myself on his mercy."

- "When I feel a great deal of stress, it makes me run to the Lord and cry out, 'God, I can't do this. I'm in over my head.'"

- "Stress disabuses you of the notion that you're in control. It drives you to intimacy with God and to trust in Him. That's a huge positive. It puts you in the Word and makes you utterly dependent on God's grace to get you through it. So, yeah, if it doesn't kill you, it makes you stronger. When you feel disappointed, or drained, or just wiped out, engage the Word. The Word of God is a creative force like none other. Let the stress drive you deeper into the Word and enhance your walk with God."

- "Worship has been primary for me in helping me through my stress. I thrive on being with God's people in worship."

- "Giving my mornings to God has been the game-changer in dealing with stress. I take very seriously that time with God. . . .That's where God brings order to my life. I pray through my day. I pray through my life. Every year, I read through the Bible and I let God speak to me.. I've done that since 1990. I also keep the discipline of journaling a prayer to God every day at the end of my time with the Lord."

This is what the apostle Paul meant when talking about his "thorn in the flesh," he said, "This is why, for Christ's sake, I delight in weaknesses, in insults, in hardships, in persecutions, in difficulties. For when I am weak, then I am strong." (2 Corinthians 12:10, NIV)

STRESS CAN STRENGTHEN A MARRIAGE.

We wince as we watch stress pull apart so many couples in ministry. I want you to know it doesn't have to be that way. Strains and tensions can, if you let them, drive you and your wife together and foster teamwork and intimacy in your marriage. Instead of making you adversaries, stress can make you allies . . . *if you let it.*

One pastor described how severe stress put him in a serious faith crisis . . . and then revealed to him what a great wife God had given him:

"I found my mind asking questions like *Does God even exist?* I wanted to walk with Christ even as I was wondering *How do I know Jesus was historical? How do I know he rose from the dead?* I wanted to minister and disciple others using God's Word even as I was thinking *How do I know this is God's Word?*

"I was living in all that tension, and one day I looked at my wife and said, 'Sweetheart, I'm afraid I'm going to end up in a rubber room.' And I'll never forget what she said, 'If they put you in a rubber room, have no fear. I'll move in there with you!' I still get emotional thinking about that moment."

STRESS CAN TEACH YOU IMPORTANT LESSONS.

Hard experiences leave scars, but they leave other things too. Mostly insight and wisdom (if we'll only keep our eyes, ears, and hearts open). Wise pastors learn important lessons from the stress in their lives. Said one:

"I don't think every time I went through a trial I necessarily got more spiritual. Sometimes I just got mad, just totally frustrated. But I would say, in general, I learned a lot of life lessons through the trials."

Another echoed that thought, "I think I learned important life lessons through the stressful times. They were painful, but I learned some things that otherwise I never would have learned. I do believe we learn our greatest lessons not when we win but when we lose."

STRESS CAN BRING OUT THE BEST IN YOU.

Think of your favorite movies. They all involve a character that wants something. However, the "hero" doesn't get that thing quickly or easily. Jason Bourne doesn't figure out his identity by doing a 10 second Google search. That would be a short and terrible movie!

Always, to defeat the bad guys or get the girl or save the world, the hero is forced to confront and overcome a series of hard obstacles. Sometimes it's brutal to watch him scratch and claw and fight. Often he suffers one setback, failure, or heartbreak after another.

But here's the truth. It wouldn't be a great story without the main character having to face and overcome hardships. By the end of all our favorite movies, not only has the hero achieved his goal at last but he's also grown and changed because of these trials. He's a different person, a better version of himself.

That's what stress can do in the life of a pastor.

And that's why pastors need what Angela Duckworth calls "grit." As she sees it, "Many of us, it seems, quit what we start far too early and far too often. Even more than the effort a gritty person puts in on a single day, what matters is that they wake up the next day, and the next, ready to get on that treadmill and keep going."[6]

Some pastors show grit—and deal with stress—by remembering their calling. Listen to one pastor who felt called to broken churches in trauma, "Part of what kept me here and kept me *from* submitting my letter of resignation is that I really had a sense that God had called me to churches that needed to be fixed. That's the kind of church I'm built for."

It's important to remember that God has put you where you are for a reason. The stress might be uncomfortable, but your calling is worthwhile. It is worth it to persevere. God will work through you and in you.

One man told me a horrific story of being maligned and mistreated by people within the church that he'd been pastoring only a few short years. The animosity grew to the point that the leaders called a business meeting with the intention of firing him. This is how he recalled that night to me:

> Before the service, I was almost hyperventilating. My heart was going about 120 miles per hour. Sweat was pouring down my face. When I put my hand on the door to go face my divided

congregation, a verse from Psalm 56 came to my mind, "This I know, God is for me."

At that moment, in my heart, God whispered, "They may fire you, but they didn't hire you." And instantly a peace came over my mind. I said to the Lord, "If they keep me, fine, if they fire me, fine. No matter what happens, you called me, I'm going to trust you and serve you."

"So help me, I felt my blood pressure and heart rate go normal, and my sweat glands dried up! I went out and preached. We were in 1 John, and it happened to be the passage, how can you say you love God, when you hate your brother. We had seven people saved that night! When the meeting was over, a move to dismiss me was never brought up. In fact, the night ended with an affirming, standing ovation for 7 minutes!

A few people left the church in the ensuing weeks, but many more came. In fact, the most fruitful years of my ministry came right after that miserable experience." Did you hear that?!? One of the repeating themes that you will resound throughout this book is that often times, pastors leave too early. When ministry becomes difficult it often seems like a losing battle and we can easily convince ourselves that it would be better for us somewhere else. But the wisdom I kept hearing repeatedly (and I will throw my own "Amen" in there from personal experience) is that the most fruitful ministry often comes after the most difficult battles and conflicts. As one pastor said to me, "Don't quit before you are finished!"

STRESS CAN GIVE YOU A HEALTHY PERSPECTIVE.

In this chapter, we've been looking at the upside of stress in the lives of pastors. We have to mention the way it gives us perspective. Stress keeps up in touch with important realities, like:

1. **Life is stressful.** I should note that all the pastors I've quoted here started in small churches. It is easy to assume that because many are now in large churches, even megachurches, their situations are different than ours. But the research shows that as the size of the church increases, the stress levels increase as well. One of them put it this way, "Stress is inevitable. Expect it. This won't change with the passage of time, either. When I first came to this church, we had 200 people, and it was stressful. Now we have a lot more people and it is even *more* stressful."

    In short: Life is stressful, and stress will always be present in various forms and in to varying degrees until heaven. It is something we have to expect and plan for!

2. **Stressors come and go.** One pastor noted, "In ministry, the way to hang in there long-term is by thinking bigger than the particular tough situation you find yourself in. You have to remember your current stress isn't going to be permanent."

    Said another, "Many pastors and spiritual leaders whine because they are in a tough season, but they don't see it as a season. They see it as, 'This is going to be my life forever and ever and ever as long as I stay at this church.'"

    That's the trouble with whining. It fails to honor stressful seasons for what they are—a season. Without this perspective, one could be overcome with anxiety and even depression, thinking, "Things will always be like this, nothing will ever change, I might as well leave." Hear the words of the wise pastor who said, "Stress does not last forever. Stick around long enough and that will become abundantly clear."

(Having said that, I should also point out that after your current stress passes, another will arise to take its place.)

3. **A little stress can be a good thing.** As mentioned earlier, there is such a thing as positive stress. Not all the pressure we face as pastors is bad for us. Unlike disturbing situations (which provoke *distress*), some challenging situations (such as work assignments that allow for autonomy and innovation) can bring on *eustress*. Eustress has positive effects on health, wellbeing, and productivity. In other words, a certain amount of stress is actually good for you.[7]

To summarize, stress gets mostly bad press. But handled correctly, it has some real benefits. It can drive you to Christ. It can strengthen your marriage. It can teach you lessons in wisdom. It can bring out the best in you—shaping your character. (That's why you can give thanks *in the middle of* it—it's making you more like Jesus!) Finally, it can give you a healthy perspective on life and ministry in a fallen world.

Stress has an upside. But we first need to recognize it and handle it correctly. More on that in the next chapter.

QUESTIONS FOR REFLECTION AND DISCUSSION

- Would you say you entered ministry with your eyes open to the stress awaiting you?

- What surprised you when you were first starting in ministry?

- Does the concept of 'positive stress' seem odd to you?

- In what ways has stress "driven you to Christ"?

- In general, how do you react when unexpected stress appears? Do you feel like it is helping to make you more like Christ? Why or why not?

- How, up to this point, has stress affected your marriage?

- What's one good lesson you've learned from a stressful experience?

- How many seasons of stress have you experienced in ministry? How long did they last?

CHAPTER 4
What's Got You So Stressed Out?

Let's don't beat around the bush here. Let's just get right to it:

What's causing *you* the most stress right now?

To recap: Stress is the pressure that produces strain in our lives. It's a force that confronts us, a burden we carry, something that weighs on us. When the pressure is severe/chronic it can be debilitating.

As we've mentioned, stress comes from all sorts of places. The pressures we face can be due to internal or external factors. They can be personal or relational, physical or financial, social or psychological. Stress can come from strain at work or strain at home. It varies in intensity.

Here's a checklist (not exhaustive) that highlights many of the common stressors ministers wrestle with. What hard situations are *you* facing right now, and how intense are they?

Factor / event	Level of Stress (i.e., intensity)
Common Church Issues	
Following a popular pastor *(maybe even the church's founding pastor)*	0 1 2 3 4 5 6 7 8 9 10
Pastoring a traumatized flock *(from a church split, moral failure, natural disaster, etc.)*	0 1 2 3 4 5 6 7 8 9 10
Strong doctrinal disagreements in the body	0 1 2 3 4 5 6 7 8 9 10
Spiritual indifference or apathy in the flock	0 1 2 3 4 5 6 7 8 9 10
Not having enough volunteers	0 1 2 3 4 5 6 7 8 9 10
Having a dis-unified board	0 1 2 3 4 5 6 7 8 9 10
Being understaffed	0 1 2 3 4 5 6 7 8 9 10
Having to deal with high-profile sin in the congregation *(i.e., church discipline)*	0 1 2 3 4 5 6 7 8 9 10
Unrealistic expectations *(on the part of the congregation)*	0 1 2 3 4 5 6 7 8 9 10

Factor / event	Level of Stress (i.e., intensity)
Common Church Issues (continued)	
Hiring new staff	0 1 2 3 4 5 6 7 8 9 10
Having to fire staff	0 1 2 3 4 5 6 7 8 9 10
The "worship wars" are raging!	0 1 2 3 4 5 6 7 8 9 10
Grumbling in the body	0 1 2 3 4 5 6 7 8 9 10
A church body that's polarized politically	0 1 2 3 4 5 6 7 8 9 10
Implementing big changes *(e.g., changing the church name; merging with another church, etc.)*	0 1 2 3 4 5 6 7 8 9 10
Not having a facility *(i.e., having to set up/break down each week)*	0 1 2 3 4 5 6 7 8 9 10
Starting a big, new program	0 1 2 3 4 5 6 7 8 9 10

Factor / event	Level of Stress (i.e., intensity)
Deciding to eliminate a long-standing program	0 1 2 3 4 5 6 7 8 9 10
Getting negative publicity in the community	0 1 2 3 4 5 6 7 8 9 10
Having to maintain an old facility	0 1 2 3 4 5 6 7 8 9 10
Needing to find property and launch a building program	0 1 2 3 4 5 6 7 8 9 10
A staff member quitting/leaving	0 1 2 3 4 5 6 7 8 9 10
Core members leaving to go to the new church	0 1 2 3 4 5 6 7 8 9 10
Following up a big ministry success	0 1 2 3 4 5 6 7 8 9 10
Overseeing a fund-raising/ stewardship campaign	0 1 2 3 4 5 6 7 8 9 10
Trying to plant a church/start a new church	0 1 2 3 4 5 6 7 8 9 10
A lack of giving leading to budget cuts	0 1 2 3 4 5 6 7 8 9 10
Dealing with an adversarial board member	0 1 2 3 4 5 6 7 8 9 10
Not seeing eye to eye with an associate	0 1 2 3 4 5 6 7 8 9 10
Having to shepherd lots of people in crisis	0 1 2 3 4 5 6 7 8 9 10
A *change* in job description (or an *ambiguous* job description)	0 1 2 3 4 5 6 7 8 9 10
The weekly pressure of preaching	0 1 2 3 4 5 6 7 8 9 10
Factions on the staff	0 1 2 3 4 5 6 7 8 9 10
Getting wind that your job might be on the line	0 1 2 3 4 5 6 7 8 9 10

Common Domestic Situations

Trying to get by on a meager salary	0 1 2 3 4 5 6 7 8 9 10
Marital discord	0 1 2 3 4 5 6 7 8 9 10

Factor / event — **Level of Stress (i.e., intensity)**

Common Domestic Situations (continued)

Wife feeling the pressure of ministry expectations	0 1 2 3 4 5 6 7 8 9 10
Living far from extended family	0 1 2 3 4 5 6 7 8 9 10
Children not flourishing	0 1 2 3 4 5 6 7 8 9 10
Children acting out	0 1 2 3 4 5 6 7 8 9 10
Older kids struggling spiritually	0 1 2 3 4 5 6 7 8 9 10
Family health struggles	0 1 2 3 4 5 6 7 8 9 10
Having to care for aging parents	0 1 2 3 4 5 6 7 8 9 10

Personal / Emotional Issues	
Workaholic patterns	0 1 2 3 4 5 6 7 8 9 10
A perfectionistic personality	0 1 2 3 4 5 6 7 8 9 10
A need to control others and/or outcomes	0 1 2 3 4 5 6 7 8 9 10
A penchant for trying to rescue/save people	0 1 2 3 4 5 6 7 8 9 10
A lack of close friendships / feelings of isolation and loneliness	0 1 2 3 4 5 6 7 8 9 10
People-pleasing tendencies	0 1 2 3 4 5 6 7 8 9 10
A lack of boundaries (i.e., the unwillingness to say no)	0 1 2 3 4 5 6 7 8 9 10
Not having a hobby or healthy outlet for R & R	0 1 2 3 4 5 6 7 8 9 10
The inability to "get away" and take breaks	0 1 2 3 4 5 6 7 8 9 10

WHY ARE PASTORS AT SUCH RISK?

Helping professionals (i.e., counselors, psychologists, social workers, and pastors) typically have strong motivations to help others. Oftentimes they get their identity from a sense of accomplishment: Did my clients have a breakthrough? Is the marriage better? Has the person's depression lifted?

Interestingly, those who enter helping professions with higher levels of optimism are often the most vulnerable to disillusionment. Pastors who enter vocational ministry without being aware of the challenges that await them are more susceptible to burnout. And if you enter ministry thinking you are about to change the world… the odds are *really* high you'll burn out.

You can see why pastors are so vulnerable, can't you? How many of us resonate with the mission to help others find God? How much are our identities unhealthily tied to success in ministry? *If I can't help lead this wayward soul back to God, then what good am I? In a city this large, surely I can grow this church from 250 to 500 in a few years.* It makes sense, then, why pastors are especially susceptible to burnout.[8]

- Fifty-four percent of pastors feel the demands of ministry are overwhelming.

- Eight out of ten feel they are on call twenty-four hours a day.

- One out of five feels that the church has placed unrealistic demands on them.

- One out of three feels isolated.

Of course, pastors are burning out! Who could ever bear all the weight of this job?

It's not surprising that so many think it best to just quit or move on to the next church where things will be better. Both are common responses to stress. Have you felt tempted to try your luck at another church? Many pastors do. However, your stress will follow you. You won't successfully cope with stress in your second church if you never learned to cope with it in your first church.

Let's highlight one other kind of stress we've mentioned:

THE STRESS OF SUCCESS

Pastors experience stress in all sorts of ways and from all kinds of sources. And, stress often comes when we least expect it. As one pastor told me, "Stress is a funny thing. It usually doesn't hit me while I'm going through a difficult time. It often comes a little later. In my life, it seems like stress is always delayed. Or, at least the results of it are."

To exacerbate the problem, stress also comes at unexpected times. A wise old minister observed, "There are two times in life when you're the most vulnerable to stress. One is when you're deeply discouraged, and the other is when you're highly successful."

We get his first point. That's obvious. It's his second point that we need to emphasize. We assume failure equals stress and success equals a hassle-free life. However, for many pastors, stress hits harder during seasons of success. Said one pastor, "When everything is humming along, there's this enormous pressure to 'keep it going.' You think *I can't have a bad sermon. We can't afford to see attendance drop.* You constantly wonder *Are we doing as well as we did last year?*"

My point? Stress is sneaky! It comes when you least expect it. And it hardly ever makes sense in the moment. It takes real effort to unravel and understand the roots of stress.

I personally think most pastoral stress comes from three sources: (1) Being spiritually and/or emotionally unhealthy; (2) Seeking fulfillment in the wrong places; and (3) Having a board, or a congregation, or a job description that places excessive demands and unrealistic expectations on us.

Unrecognized, stress from these places inhibits our ability to fulfill our duties, enjoy healthy relationships, and maintain our own personal health. Unchecked, this kind of relentless pressure will lead to burnout.

Two other key stressors contributing to pastoral burnout are isolation and loneliness.[9] Most pastors experience feelings of loneliness and isolation because of the unique demands of their jobs. One put it this way,

"The more stressed and exhausted I felt, the more I wanted to retreat and avoid people. But God made us so that we need others. It's right there in the opening pages of Scripture—it's not good for man to be alone. I think life gets even harder and more stressful when you're not in community. And I believe deep friendships can keep you sane."

The prophet Elijah is a prime example of this. Do you remember when he, faced off against the 800+ prophets of Baal and Ashura on Mt. Carmel?

We see this strong picture of Elijah—he is the only one representing Yahweh. And he not only confronts these false prophets that are serving false gods, but he also engages in some serious taunting! At one point he tells them that maybe they should cry out a little louder since it's possible their god is sitting on the toilet! God used Elijah that day to secure a decisive victory against the forces that sought to take Israel deep into idolatry and rebellion.

However, after this incredible display of God's power and Elijah's boldness, following one threat from Jezebel, Elijah seems to run for his life. I have often heard preachers suggest that Elijah ran in fear. But the text doesn't lend itself to that interpretation, either contextually or grammatically.

Elijah doesn't run because he is scared, he runs because he is tired. In fact, it's his tired condition that has convinced him he is the only one who doesn't bow the knee to these false gods, and he probably will always be the only one. God has to intervene in Elijah's thought process to get him back to a good mental state. He first gives him some food and rest, and then he gently reminds him that he is not the only one—there are many in Israel who have not bowed the knee to Baal or Ashura. And he also tells him that he is sending him a companion and his eventual replacement in the person of Elisha.

Here's a reminder of why it's critical for pastors to build and sustain close and supportive relationships with others. Good friendships make us resilient in the face of stress. If we lose a grasp on our relationships or on our humanity, we are in serious trouble. We'll discuss this more in the pages that follow.

QUESTIONS FOR REFLECTION AND DISCUSSION

- Do you know any pastors who have experienced the pain of burnout? Were you surprised by their experience?

- What did you notice as you worked through the chart/ checklist on common pastoral stressors? Did anything surprise or alarm you?

- Do you typically experience more stress at church or at home?

- Do you feel on call twenty-four hours a day? Are you over-whelmed? Do think you face unrealistic demands?

- How many of the personal/emotional stressors cited do you bat-tle on a regular basis?

- Do you ever feel lonely in ministry/life? And if so, what do you do to combat that?

- Do you agree that success can be stressful in its own unique way? Why or why not? When have you experienced this?

CHAPTER 5
It Came from Within!

When your pastoral stress levels are off the charts, it's easy to point the finger. We can blame "that stubborn board member" or "this impossible job description." Then, if we're not careful, we can unknowingly slip into victim mode. Suddenly we're "that poor clergy guy" who's at the mercy of people and events.

To be fair, that *is* sometimes an accurate picture of reality. People *can* be jerks, and situations often *are* brutal. But too often we skim past another uncomfortable truth, which is:

> **Many of the stressors that wreck us don't come**
> **from without; they come from within.**

Let me say that again, in another way. *Sometimes the real reason we're miserable has less to do with external factors and more to do with internal, personal realities—the way we're wired, and the unhealthy tendencies we've embraced.*

Let me explain what I mean through a series of questions.

WHAT'S YOUR PERSONALITY TYPE?

In general, being a "people person" is a boon to anyone in vocational ministry. Being extroverted and outgoing can be an advantage for a pastor. Why? Because the typical pastoral role requires interacting with people *much of the time*. Those who are highly relational don't get as stressed when they have to engage socially. In fact, they usually get energized.

Am I saying extroversion is a *requirement* for pastors? Or that ministers need to be able to "work a room" and "press the flesh" like a politician? No. I'm simply saying that being outgoing is an *advantage* when you're called to care for people.

But it's not *necessary*. Something one pastor said in his interview stands out. "We are serving a God of grace, who provides strength in our weakness. You don't have to be a social butterfly or a psychoanalyst to be a pastor. Even those who struggle in this area can thrive in ministry."

It's been said that introverts make up 33-40 percent of the population. (Perhaps the same percentage applies to those in ministry?) Whatever the precise number, introverts definitely need more downtime, more time alone for reflection. They get energized by solitude—and stressed when forced to be with people and in groups constantly.

If you're a more introverted pastor, you can reduce your stress by being wise and careful in how you schedule your days. Be sure to make time for solitude.

Another pastor elaborated on the role that one's *personality type* plays in ministry.

> "My personality type is that of the peacemaker. I guess that's an "S" on the Performax/DiSC test or a 9 if you're into the Enneagram. Anyway, my point is I tend to get anxious and stressed whenever I sense tension, whenever I can tell people are upset with me or with each other. And, of course, in church world, there's almost *always* tension! You can't avoid it.

But just knowing my tendencies—because of my unique personality—is a big help."

ARE YOU CARRYING AROUND BAGGAGE FROM YOUR CHILDHOOD?

Regardless of one's personality type, dealing with people is often stressful. Sometimes, however, the roots of our interpersonal struggles are *internal*. In other words, the stress you're feeling in interacting with others might be more of a "you" problem rather than a "them" problem. And some of those issues might be traceable all the way back to your childhood and your family of origin.

Studies suggest that the helping professions (like ministry) often attract individuals whose childhoods were spent trying to satisfy the high expectations of their parents, but whose emotional needs went unmet. Such people often carry this behavior pattern into adulthood, attempting to gain a sense of self-worth from fulfilling the needs of others.

Put bluntly, many pastors have self-esteem issues. They hope to feel worthy and valuable by showing compassion and helping others—and getting attention, approval, and affection in return. When this doesn't work, some attempt to fulfill those longings through inappropriate behavior. Thus, all kinds of behaviors can be driven by issues surrounding self-esteem. When a leader becomes obsessed with satisfying an endless and enormous need for approval, it often leads to stress and burnout.[10] Pastors with this kind of background crave admiration and acclaim. It can become a kind of addiction.

ARE YOU A PEOPLE PLEASER?

Often connected to the search for self-esteem is the internal mindset that says: *I can't ever say or do anything that will upset anyone because I need everyone to like me.*

A retired pastor admitted:

"It's exhausting trying to please everyone. When our church merged with another congregation, we had duplicate staff. Obviously, we couldn't afford two youth pastors, two worship pastors, etc. We had to make some hard choices.

"I learned that leadership is like being a sports referee. Half the people are mad at you no matter what call you make! I had to remind myself constantly that I'm only responsible for my choices, not for how people react to my choices."

People pleasers are always nice and agreeable. But really, this behavior is self-centered. And it's deadly in ministry. It's not your job to make people happy. You're called to honor God and love people. And often loving people involves saying words and taking actions they won't like.

DO YOU TEND TO BE PERFECTIONISTIC?

Perfectionism is what makes Pastor Ken stay up past midnight most Saturdays, trying to get his sermon *exactly right*. (It's frankly a big reason he's teetering on the edge of burnout.) Why is he that way? Where did that come from? It's hard to say, though it's worth noting his parents *were* the kind who often grilled him about grades with questions like: "Why'd you only make a 97 and not a 100?"

Perfectionism is also what makes Brother Charles' wife Elaine agonize for *days* before she hosts any kind of church event at their home.

One pastor said, "Tying to be a perfectionist when you're woefully imperfect is a quick ticket to Crazyville. You'll end up disgusted with yourself and critical of everything and everybody. I'd say you need to get comfortable with saying, 'That's *good enough*.' Otherwise, you're not going to make it very long."

He's right. As fallen creatures in a fallen world, we're foolish to expect perfection. Think about it like this: If we could be perfect by trying really hard, why would we need God's grace? Why would we need the gospel?

ARE YOU A WORKAHOLIC?

Probably a first cousin to being a perfectionist is having a tendency toward workaholism.

You go in early. You come home late. You put in 60 or 70 hours a week—and then feel guilty that you're not doing enough.

"Just a few more minutes." "Just a little more effort." "I've got too much to do!" "If I don't do it, who will?" "There's not enough time in the day!" Ever hear yourself saying those things?

Have you ever heard someone say, "The Devil doesn't take a day off, so neither do I?" Have you ever thought that maybe that's why he's the devil?!? (Ha!)

Listen, hard work for the Lord is commendable, but an obsession with work is sick. It's a sign of a disordered heart. Remember, Jesus said, "*I* will build my church" (emphasis added). He did *not* say, "I am counting on _____ (your name here) to build my church."

Can you see how overworking is actually a form of pride? Think about sacrificing your pride for the sake of your long-term spiritual, mental, physical, and emotional health instead. No one else is going to look out for you in these areas in the ways you can. Care about yourself, or burn out. It is really as simple as that.

DO YOU HAVE A "SAVIOR COMPLEX"?

- If only this miserable married couple would heed my brilliant words of counsel…
- If only I could pray the right prayer…

- If only my board would get behind my initiative, we could turn this city upside down…

- If only my congregation would take my theologically rich sermons to heart…

- If only I could meet with that skeptic and explain the gospel to him…

One of the worst things a pastor can do is to see himself as anyone's "savior."

I'm talking about that internal, self-induced pressure that says—often subconsciously—"It's up to *me*" or "It's *my* responsibility" to fix people or rescue them. When we get in this mindset we envision ourselves as spiritual superheroes. Souls and marriages hang in the balance! And we have the power to save the day!

Except that we don't. Not really.

Solving everyone's problems is not our role. We're not saviors; we're servants *of the Savior*. We're called to love and pray and trust and preach. It's up to the Almighty to rescue and redeem and restore. Those are things only he can do. We're responsible to do our small part. He's in charge of outcomes.

In describing this common phenomenon, psychologists often draw on the work of Carl Jung. He described the so-called "Savior Complex" as a serious hazard to the mental health of psychoanalysts. (FYI, his insights apply to pastors every bit as much as psychologists.)

What we know is that those afflicted with this condition are often vulnerable to compassion fatigue, i.e., the stress that results from helping or desiring to help others who have experienced trauma or suffering.

Many people turn to their pastors as a primary source of support in times of distress or crisis. We are often called upon to minister to congregants who are terminally ill. Because of these realities, we must learn to care without being consumed. Otherwise, we will eventually succumb to the stress of secondary trauma over time.[11]

DO YOU SUFFER FROM IMPOSTER SYNDROME?

Lots of Christians want their pastors to be "experts," knowledgeable *and* conversant in every spiritual area: theology, biblical languages, church history, denominational differences, apologetics, cults, cultural issues . . . and on and on and on.

Sometimes, pastors unwittingly succumb to this pressure. They try in vain to live up to all the hype. For instance, you mention the definition of a Greek word in one of your sermons and suddenly, Sister Ethyl is online telling all her friends "My pastor is a Greek scholar."

Multiply that scenario by 100, and you can see why so many pastors are always looking over their shoulders. You ever felt like that? Of course you have! Welcome to the club, of which I am the President.

This is Imposter Syndrome, chronic anxiety you'll be found out for the fraud you believe yourself to be. You feel like a poser. You dread someone asking you a question "you're supposed to know" but you don't.

Let this charade go on and it will become chronic stress. It will eat your lunch. It will eat YOU for lunch.

DO YOU SUFFER FROM MARTYR SYNDROME?

There is a popular idea in many pastoral circles that says self-care is, well, self*ish*, and that self-sacrifice is always preferable because it's always godly.

Wrong. This kind of "spiritual stoicism" is a lie. Servanthood and self-care aren't mutually exclusive. Denying yourself good and necessary things doesn't square with the abundant life Jesus promised his followers. Friendships, sleep, great food, social gatherings, exercise, hobbies, laughter, spending time with family—these are all good gifts from above, necessary parts of a healthy, well-rounded life.

The pastor who feels compelled to continually sacrifice his mental, emotional, physical, relational, or spiritual health for "the sake of the gospel" is misguided. He should be pitied, not praised. Why? Because he's going to reap a host of not-so-pleasant consequences.

What should those who scoff at self-care expect? Higher incidence of physical illness, relational strain, spiritual dissatisfaction, and emotional trauma.

In short, such pastors are on the fast track to burnout.

HAVE YOU EMBRACED UNREALISTIC EXPECTATIONS?

Many of us experience needless stress because we're carrying around unrealistic expectations. Here's what I mean. You *expect* something—a church service, a sermon, a meeting, a restaurant, a movie, whatever—to be at least an "8" or "9" on the old 1-10 scale. But then it turns out to be only a "5" or a "6". Ugh. That difference, between what you expected and what you experienced, is the degree to which you end up feeling disappointed.

Without even thinking, we create expectations about most things. However, by learning to notice and adjust our expectations, we can avoid the stress of unnecessary disappointment. As one pastor said,

> "One of my coping mechanisms for dealing with stress is that
> I lower my expectations of people. If you go into a relation-
> ship not *expecting* people to be loyal, not expecting someone
> to always do the right thing, then when they actually do, it's
> all the better."

Sounds cynical, maybe, but it is also being realistic And it's not just people, we can also embrace unrealistic expectations of ministry in general.

One study revealed a *big* gap between most pastors' expectations of ministry before entering it and the ministerial realities they actually encountered.

Maybe you can relate. You showed up with your seminary degree and all your theological insight. You were going to turn that church and town upside down. Then reality smacked you in the face.

Or you attended the big church conference and took copious notes. You came home and did all the things the celebrity pastor of that booming megachurch said *he* did. You just *knew* it was going to change everything. Then reality punched you in the throat.

Hey, it's fine to *hope* for good things. And it's right to *trust* God for big things. But when it comes to expectations, be smart. Embracing unrealistic ones will lead to dissatisfaction, a limited sense of joy, and a loss of meaning and calling.[12]

IS YOUR TRAINING DEFICIENT?

Surveys indicate that many pastors feel ill-equipped in the areas of *management* and *leadership*. They studied the Bible, theology, Greek and Hebrew, and preaching in their seminary courses, but many never received any training in how to lead an organization. These personal inadequacies can weigh heavily on a pastor's soul (or mess with his head, however you want to phrase it.)

New pastors are often shocked by the extent of managerial and leadership duties their vocation demands, and by how poorly their formal training prepared them for these aspects of ministry.

Most of us see ourselves as spiritual leaders, not organizational managers—despite the reality that successful church ministry entails the performance of managerial and administrative tasks. [13]

Many studies—and experts—now recommend more extensive training in conflict management, team building, collaborative decision-making, emotional intelligence, and agenda-setting. These are invaluable for enhancing ministers' interpersonal skills. They're crucial for someone leading an organization.[14] The pastors in my study had these skills and used them constantly.

QUESTIONS FOR REFLECTION AND DISCUSSION

- Do you agree that much pastoral stress comes from within? Why or why not?

- Have you taken any personality tests, and if so, what have you learned about how your personality makes you susceptible, or impervious, to various stressors?

- Talk about your childhood—specifically the expectations your parents had of you, and how well they met your emotional needs."

- On a scale of 1-10, with 1 being "not at all" and 10 being "I'm hopeless," how much of a people pleaser are you?

- What does the "Savior Complex" mean to you? How much of a problem is this for you?

- Would you say you entered ministry with realistic expectations? If not what surprised and/or disappointed you?

- Where are you on the scale from extreme self-care to extreme self-sacrifice?

- Would the people closest to you ever call you a *perfectionist*? What about a *workaholic*?

- Do you feel adequately trained? If not, what skills would be most helpful for you to learn?

CHAPTER 6
Those Pesky People

"Ministry would be the greatest job in the world," Brother Charles said last week, before pausing and adding, "if it weren't for all those pesky people."

Even though it's an old joke, we laugh. He's right. It's true. People make ministry messy and stressful. And yet ministry is *all about people*.

I heard a story about a pastor who was walking down the hallway early one Sunday morning when he spotted Sister Ethyl way down the corridor, heading in his direction. He was in no mood to hear about all the things wrong with the church and everything he should be doing. So...

Before she could spot him, the pastor ducked into a dark classroom. As he rushed into the room he tripped over three deacons who were already squatting down on the floor.

"What are y'all doing in here?" the pastor asked. The men responded, "The same thing you are... avoiding Sister Ethyl!" The pastor shook his head, "That's ridiculous! Go out there and be nice to that lady." The deacons responded, "No sir, you go be nice to her... you're the minister. You're paid to be good. We're good for nothing."

Funny, but familiar!

So what's a pastor to do? How can we get better at navigating the "people stressors" of ministry?

Listen to what one pastor said:

"My first go-round in ministry was a disaster. I didn't like being around church people. I left church work, became a functional alcoholic, and went into the business world, where I was very successful. But I was miserable.

"When God gave me a second chance, I came back with a completely new attitude and a lot of humility. I admitted, 'God, I don't know how to deal with people. That was part of my downfall before. You're going to have to teach me how to understand people, their nature, and who they are.'

"My failure taught me a lot about grace. That was the biggest thing—the fact that God would be patient with me and restore me, and that God would allow me to do something sacred after all I had done. I didn't deserve that. It was a great lesson for a pastor about being merciful to others."

Being constantly blown away by God's grace for us—and then showing that same grace to others . . . think *that* would solve most, if not all, our people irritations?

But since we're not always so grace-full, let's go ahead and take a quick look at some specific and common "people issues" that create stress for pastors. We'll consider two groups broadly: church people and staff people.

ISSUES WITH CHURCH MEMBERS

A common source of stress mentioned in my conversations with veteran clergy was *unhappy church members*. Six of the ten pastors who cited this factor said upset church members are a *major* stress to them. One explicitly said *unhappy church members* are his greatest stress.

No doubt, every pastor needs the wise reminder of the pastor who said, "It's doesn't take many to make a lot of noise... two bullfrogs croaking in a millpond on Saturday night can sound like 100! You have to keep in mind it's rarely as many as you think."

Stressors with church people—where do they arise? Truth be told, they can stem from all sorts of things:

Pastoral transitions. A new pastor experiences relational tension because church members are still fiercely loyal to the previous pastor. People are grieving his departure. Meanwhile, the new minister up the road a bit catches flak because church members are still angry at the pastor who just left! Crazy, right? Church members taking out their frustrations on the innocent new guy who hasn't done anything wrong? Yet it happens. All the time.

Personal issues. One pastor observed that his "people stress" always came from two related sources: church members who were upset with and at him and those *who were floundering in their own messy lives.* He said:

> "There's a stress that comes from those who are antagonistic toward your ministry. They want to embarrass you, hurt you, smear you, and compromise you in the eyes of others. That's one type, and it's ugly. It hurts. Then there's another kind of stress that comes when I know I could help someone, but they won't accept help. They just stay stuck. And that stress might actually break my heart even more."

It's important to remember that much of a church member's unhappiness often has little or nothing to do with you. Many times it stems from them being *disgruntled, upset, angry,* or *hurt* in their own lives. It just leaks out. You know the old saying, "Hurt people hurt people"? It's true. Unhappy people spread unhappiness.

Unrealistic expectations. Other pastors discussed feeling the people stress that arises from *expectations*, specifically the high expectations church members have for pastors.

"When you're unable to accomplish the goals members of the church put on you, it can weigh on you. Some people expect a lot from you and there's a sense of inadequacy. You're aware of your vulnerabilities and weaknesses, and you know you can't reach their expected standard. And often this affects the way they treat you."

Human irrationality. One pastor I talked with suggested that some of our people stress might arise from the fact that people aren't always rational:

"I think every church is allotted a certain number of crazy people. (We happen to have an extra allotment from the Lord. And so we have craziness all the time!) More people equal more problems. Such is life in the church. The good news is this: God hasn't called you or me or anybody else to fix people; he just calls us to love them."

Scorekeeping. What about when folks in the flock become petty? They get mad at you because you visited so-and-so's mother in the hospital, but you didn't visit their mother. If you've experienced that, you know people can say and do cruel and vindictive things.

Those are precisely the times we need to guard against getting down on their level. It's tempting to want to keep score right back—hold on to those wrongs others have done instead of forgiving them.

Don't do it. Speaking of this temptation, one pastor warned, "If you're going to keep score, ministry is not the place for you. Thinking *I did more for them than they did for me!*—that ain't ministry."

Others also cautioned against this. One put it quite vividly, "I have found in so many relationships people think, 'I do two things for you, you do two things for me.' It's almost like relational poker, and I just don't play that. I just help people and expect nothing in return. It actually makes it nice, because you're never disappointed since you weren't expecting anything."

Criticism and negativity. What about extremely critical parishioners? Got any folks like that? One pastor told this wild story:

"I had a man in my church who was always negative. One day, I had the opportunity to go canoeing with him as I was beginning to build a relationship with him. On that trip, I asked him, 'Why are you always so negative about things? Tell me about that.'

"'Well,' he said, 'I just feel like God wants me to look at the other side of things and offer another viewpoint.' He went on to say, 'I actually voted against you coming to be our new pastor. I wasn't against you, I just figured if one negative vote would cause you not to come, you probably shouldn't come.'

(I think that guy must belong to a *lot* of churches! Every pastor I know of seems to have one or more members just like him.)

Without a doubt, this kind of contrarian member feels more like a curse than a blessing. But, what if we chose—with God's help—to see such people as blessings in disguise? A different point of view *can* sometimes move a discussion—or a body—forward in ways we couldn't have imagined.

Stubborn sheep! Younger pastors often get impatient and frustrated because people won't quickly follow their lead. They forget that following requires a great deal of trust. One of the pastors I interviewed said, "You have to earn people's trust; they have to get to the point where they believe you."

Another echoed that idea, "People problems lessen when you earn the right to be their pastor. That usually takes three to five years, in my opinion. Once you do that, the really fruitful ministry begins."

He brings up a good point. Of all the pastors I surveyed, a common theme seemed to be that roughly between year five and year seven they had a major crisis within the church. They also mentioned that their most fruitful years in ministry came right after that crisis.

The reason this is important is that the precedent literature says that most pastors only stay at a church for around five years. Could it be that a crisis or a looming crisis is what prompts many to leave? And could it be that leaving is why some miss out on incredibly fruitful times in ministry?

That's brings us to . . .

Traumas and crisis. We said it already, but it bears repeating: ministry is hard. On the day of our interview, one pastor told me:

"This morning, about 6:15, I get a call about an attempted suicide. And so I am dealing with the family back and forth. Then another lady calls and she is widowed about six months now, and really struggling... And so, I am hands-on, ministering to these people for a big chunk of my day. That can drain you, you know? You can only give out so much."

Ministering to people in pain can introduce stress into a pastor's life, putting him in danger of *compassion fatigue.* Recall what we said earlier: compassion fatigue is what you feel when you begin taking on the secondary stress of others in unhealthy ways. Over time, ironically, this deep compassion for people can lead to a lack of compassion—an inability to care deeply!

One pastor talked about his struggles on this slippery slope:

"I feel with my people, I hurt with my people, I weep with my people. I have a tendency to make myself sick to make you well. There will be a lot of people at my funeral, but that funeral may come early... Sometimes I almost kill myself trying to serve and please others!"

Can you relate? Such feelings are far more common than you might suspect. This is a regular challenge for those in helping professions.

Meaning, we have to find the balance between compassion for others and care for ourselves.

Given how vulnerable pastors often are to compassion fatigue, it may seem surprising that only two of the pastors I interviewed mentioned this particular "people stress." Probably this was due to age. Compassion fatigue is far more likely to impact new or younger ministers. In fact, it is a leading factor in their burnout.[15]

However, it's not only people in the pews that make life stressful for pastors. The people in the offices on either side of us can create drama too.

ISSUES WITH STAFF PEOPLE

We could probably write a whole book on this topic alone. Maybe even a series of books?

For now, let's just briefly mention a few realities about staff teams.

Staff teams are always flawed. Before Pastor Ken fires his youth pastor Ryan, maybe he needs to hear this thought from one of the pastors I spoke with:

> "A lot of the pastoral stress that I've faced through the years has come from working with the church staff. Whenever I have issues with staff, I am always comforted by the fact that Jesus handpicked twelve associates, and out of those twelve, Judas betrayed him, Peter denied him, and Thomas doubted him. The others all had other issues. That gives me comfort. If this happened to Jesus, who am I to think it won't happen to me?"

(And I would add, it's not just staff *teams* that are flawed. So is every staff *leader*.)

Every staff has a history. One pastor I talked with said some of the tension between him and other staff members was because they had been hired by a previous pastor.

Unless you're planting a brand-new church, you may find yourself in the same situation—working with staff members who were already in their positions before you showed up. They remember how things used to be. They're accustomed to doing things "the way I/we have always done them."

The wise pastor will need to find creative ways to relate to these folks. They have established ways of going about their jobs. You'll need to take the time to earn their trust just as you would the larger congregation.

Staff communication is always a challenge. One pastor reported that miscommunication was at the root of nearly all of his problems with his church staff. "In all the years I've been pastor, I've learned that most of the time, when staff relations aren't great, it's due to miscommunication."

Another pastor agreed, noting how new technologies that are supposed to enhance communication often create more misunderstanding:

"Communication has always been stressful. I think email and text messaging have exacerbated this stress. We think technology has made life easier. I think it makes it trickier in a lot of different ways. It's important to always be asking, 'Am I being understood correctly here?'"

He raises a valid point. How many times a week do emails get misread or texts make things less clear? We're rarely able to communicate clearly and effectively through these electronic means.

Said another pastor who was frustrated by staff members whose faces were often buried in their smartphones, "I've had staff meetings where I wanted to grab some phones and throw them through the wall! Connect people? More like *disconnect* people from each other and from reality!"

Every staff team has a unique work ethic. One pastor talked about slacking staff members adding stress to his own job. "If I have staff members who are not carrying their part of the load, whether it's music, or education, or whatever, that puts stress on me because now I am going to have to pump that ministry up somehow or other."

Another pastor echoed this idea:

"There's definite stress from having to deal with staff that are not as 'Go get 'em!' as you are. Some of my staff I inherited. I didn't hire them, and they weren't sure they wanted me around. Early on, that was a source of some real stress. Since then, there have been one or two others I've brought in that I've had to deal with. You just want your staff to be on the team and to work hard. And you feel it reflects on you when they're not. That's stressful."

Firing staff is tough. A pastor of a megachurch said his greatest "staff stress" comes when he realizes one of them needs to go. "Those have been the hardest decisions, the most stressful times of my ministry life. But sometimes you have to let staff members go when they do not fit the team."

This comes at a cost. Consider what this pastor endured during his stressful season:

"I let twenty-three people go and faced seven lawsuits during my first two years at the church. But I came out of all that with a blessing, because after those two years I gained the trust of a lot of people. They thought, 'My gosh, the guy's made of Teflon!' So, I think I gained a lot of respect there, and I was able to ride that wave of trust for a long time."

A pastor of a smaller congregation told a story of demoting a staff member:

"We had a beloved worship pastor. Classic 'nice guy.' Extremely talented. But he had several side gigs. And he piddled around in the office, operated on autopilot, and probably only worked about 20 hours a week. We confronted him and nothing changed. When we finally said, 'If you're only going to work part-time, we're only going to pay you part-time,' the congregation revolted. By their reaction, you'd have thought we were advocating child sacrifice or something!"

This is news to exactly no one, but relationships—even among believers—are messy and uncomfortable. Pastors experience the stressors that come from working with people, both in the church body and on the church staff.

These reflections and anecdotes have no doubt brought to mind your own stressful relationships. The details vary but many of the dynamics are the same.

Perhaps it would do us all good to talk through some of our people experiences?

QUESTIONS FOR REFLECTION / DISCUSSION

- Do you have any prominent memories of unhappy church members? What happened?

- If you replaced a pastor when you started, did you experience tension because of it?

- How do you typically handle it when church members are upset with you?

- Do you sense that some church members have expectations of you that you can't meet?

- Do you ever find yourself "keeping score" in ministry?

- Were there existing staff members in place when you started at the church where you now serve? What was that transition like?

- To what degree have you experienced tension with church members and/or staff over the way they "used to do things"?

- What's the worst instance of miscommunication you've experienced while in ministry?

- What role does technology play in your staff communications? Has this ever caused problems?

- If you ever had to let staff go, what was that experience like?

CHAPTER 7

"Organized Religion"

An oxymoron is a figure of speech made up of two paradoxical or seemingly contradictory terms. The word itself—*oxymoron*—comes from two Greek words that together literally mean "sharp stupid."

We preachers use oxymorons all the time.

At lunch yesterday, Pastor Ken lamented to his wife about how the congregation is "growing smaller." At supper, he beamed as he told his son that his grades are "awfully good."

Brother Charles said today he's planning a "working vacation" next month. He insists this is his "only option" for getting away.

And Damian? He keeps talking about a "devout atheist" he met this week. When the man started ranting about how much he hates "organized religion," Damian smiled and told him, "Well, come to our church then. You'll love it. We're the most disorganized group in town."

Let's spend a few minutes thinking about the paradox of "organized religion." *Specifically, let's mention some of the ways organizational issues create stress for pastors.*

ORGANIZING ANY SORT OF ORGANIZATION IS STRESSFUL.

Of the twenty pastors I interviewed for my dissertation, eleven were adamant that the *organizational aspects* of the church created stress for them. They cited "the structural, logistical, and administrative aspects of running a church" and admitted these take "a heavy toll" on pastors.

One of the smartest things I ever did, I did almost by accident. I hired an administrative pastor.

Now, understand, we were a new church plant. Nobody was getting paid. I didn't have the money to hire an administrative pastor. But I knew that administration (a) was crucial, and (b) was not my gifting. If it were left up to me, the church would suffer and stagnate because of my lack of organizational skills.

So I decided that the first full-time employee of the church would NOT be me… it would be someone who was organized. That turned out to be one of the best decisions I ever made.

It allowed our growing church to avoid pandemonium and even plan for further growth, while I continued to focus on the things I was more gifted and qualified to do.

From experience, I know this to be true, and I suspect you do too. Any time people come together, even if it's just a few couples having dinner, a certain amount of organizing and planning is necessary. Otherwise, you end up with chaos.

This is especially true in the life of a church. In the early church, the apostles had to appoint deacons to take on the responsibilities of organizing and administrating (Acts 6:1-15). Before that, Jesus used the metaphors of shepherding sheep, leading and feeding a flock. (For a lot of modern pastors, the image that resonates more strongly is herding *cats*.)

Take Damian's L.A. church plant for example. When they were only 10-16 in number, they met in various homes. But as City Church grew in size, they needed more space. And there was also a growing need for more structure, for systems to keep up with all the people—and help them grow in the faith.

The leadership team of the new fellowship began batting around questions like:

- How can we build community and make disciples *between Sundays*?

- Should we utilize home groups?

- We are a prolific bunch—what are we going to do with all these kids? How can we create a great church experience for them?

- Oh, and by the way, which of us are going to agree to lead small groups and children's programs?

Questions like these prompt other questions (especially in the hearts of weary pastors who have been engaged in ministry for any length of time):

- Can the church itself—with all its activities and ministries— unwittingly contribute to the problem of pastoral burnout? In other words, do some structures make pastoral burnout more likely?

- How do we keep elaborate programs and complicated systems from becoming "larger than life" and the proverbial "tail that wags the dog"?

- How do pastors of growing churches avoid creating "organizational monsters" that chew them up and spit them out, even as they grind volunteers to the nubs?

- What if a church badly needs organization, but its pastor is bad at organization?

We know that disorganization, unclear roles, inadequate training and support, and poor communication between divisions/departments make life stressful for secular leaders. Guess what? The same issues can also create havoc and headaches in a church.

COMMON ORGANIZATIONAL STRESSORS FOR PASTORS

Church history and culture. If your organization has been around for any length of time, it has a history. That can be mostly good or bad. Usually, it's a bit of both.

Maybe you've seen God do some amazing things. I sure hope so. Celebrate those victories and blessings often.

Maybe your congregation has faced scandal or tragedy. Maybe it's suffered the pain of a church split, the moral failure of a previous minister, the lingering effects of some kind of disaster, or having to go without a minister for an extended time.

If so, you're likely to have members who are carrying around unprocessed grief or anger. Again, I think of the old saying that "hurt people hurt people"? It's true. People who are in pain (and don't process it well) typically cause a lot of pain.

This happens with pastors too. Spiritual leaders who have been wounded (and haven't responded healthily) often create a staff/church culture with systems designed to mitigate future hurt. One retired pastor said:

> "Early in my ministry, I served under a pastor who was so hyper-sensitive he wouldn't tolerate *any* opposing viewpoints. If you gently suggested an alternative idea or offered mild pushback against his ideas, you were considered disloyal and labeled as 'critical' or 'not on the team.' He wasn't aggressive in doing this—more like passive-aggressive. He would simply marginalize staffers he viewed as a 'threat' until they got so

frustrated they'd leave. Then he'd act all sad (when in truth he was relieved to have them out of his way)."

One study suggested that ministers who serve in "traumatized churches" experience greater emotional exhaustion. Interestingly, this weariness continued for some even *after* leaving their traumatic work environment. In other words, the damage stuck with them whether they were forced out or left due to relentless psychological abuse. My point is this: leaving a traumatized church does not magically stop the trauma. You cannot run from stress. A pastor can still suffer emotional exhaustion from a traumatic experience that's in his distant past.[16]

In addition to (and related to) every organization's/church's unique *history* is its *culture*. A church culture is a set of shared practices and values. It's really a way of life, a way of functioning that creates a feel. This "vibe" permeates everything—the services, the preaching, the ministries, the programs. So, for example, one church feels buttoned-up and formal. Another is laid-back and informal. One staff feels like a family. Another feels more corporate, like a business.

Whatever the culture, it affects the way the church functions. That culture also determines how stressful it is to work in. A church can have a culture that ignores conflict (perhaps due to a history with a pastor who did that). If you are a leader who addresses conflict, you will feel the stress of opposition.

One church is so relaxed it drives high capacity, high-performing staffers and members crazy. Another has a fast-paced, corporate culture that wears out more relational staff members with performance expectations and lofty ministry benchmarks.

When everything is said and done, the most contented pastors are probably those in churches that have a culture that aligns with their personality.

Scheduling. This can be another source of stress for pastors. How many events are on the church calendar, and how many are you expected to attend? Are all those programs really helping your church fulfill its mission? Or do they just give the appearance of "Look at us! We're a church that has a lot going on!"? Are you wearing out your members with too many meetings and activities? Do staff members communicate with each other to avoid overscheduling?

Could you eliminate good but not necessary programs and make church less stressful for everyone?

Structure. One pastor talked about the unhealthy ministry structure at a church he worked at before becoming a senior pastor:

> "Our senior pastor/staff director was off-the-charts 'whatever.' Because of his laissez-faire leadership style, we were less like a team pulling in the same direction and more like a bunch of independent contractors, each of us doing our own thing.

> "It was so chaotic and competitive. Everyone just went off in a corner, made a ministry plan for their 'area,' then went for it. We stayed in our individual 'ministry silos,' only coming out to compete for the best volunteers and the prime slots on the church calendar.

> "Eventually some of our more visionary (or insecure?) staff members became obsessed with, 'How can I make my ministry bigger?' They never stopped to ask (or were forced to stop and ask), 'If I create a new program that sucks up the time and energy of 200 volunteers, how is that going to affect other vital ministries?' It was a profoundly unhealthy ministry structure, and it generated a lot of unnecessary stress for everyone."

Roles. Many pastors feel organizational stress due to unclear roles and/or undefined job descriptions. Research shows that role conflict and role ambiguity can torpedo work attitudes, job satisfaction, organizational commitment, and job engagement.

Maybe you can relate. Everyone has a different idea about what you should be doing. Your spouse says you have no business volunteering to lead a men's group. The seniors think you should be doing more hospital visitation. Of your five board members, one wishes you'd do more sermon prep and counseling, another wants you leading regular, ongoing evangelistic efforts, a third wants you spending more time overseeing/training the staff, the fourth wants you out in the community more, and the fifth says "Amen" to whatever anyone else says!

No wonder you're frustrated!

Some of the pastors I talked with mentioned the stress they experienced when church growth *forced* them to change roles. One pastor lamented his inability to form and maintain personal relationships with all the new members joining his church each month. Organizationally, he finally got to the place where he had to hire someone to do outreach. This changed the nature of his job as a pastor:

> "For me, church is about relationships. So in the first ten years of our church—when we grew to about 2,000 people—I made it a goal to sit in every single visitor's living room. As a result, I could call them each by name when they walked down the aisle to join the church. Eventually, I realized that if the church continued growing at that pace, I would have to give that up. So I reluctantly hired a full-time staff person who did nothing but reach out to new people and try to assimilate them into our body. The price I paid was significant. It meant that going forward, I would *not* personally know everyone who became part of our congregation. I had no choice. But still . . . I had to give up something that I really loved."

Ouch. Talk about growing pains. On the one hand, growth is exciting—it usually means you're doing something right! But growth also necessitates change, and change is hard and stressful.

The pastor just quoted talked about this very thing:

> "I think the major organizational stressors for me have been *internal*. I went from leading a small church in a one-horse

town to overseeing a multiplicity of ministries. We now have ten or eleven full-time pastoral staff, plus another eight or ten support staff. We've got a preschool with fifty employees! I've had to navigate some serious role changes. In the beginning, I was the guy who did *everything* . . . from changing the ink cartridge in the copy machine to preaching to calling on every visitor. Now, I look around and think, 'What am I supposed to do now?'. . . It's forced a change personally, in how I see myself as a pastor."

Communication. Said one pastor, "Communication is always an issue in every organization. Whether it's two people on staff or 200, clear communication is always important. It's easy to under-communicate and equally easy to miscommunicate. Both are stressful."

Creating a culture of consistently clear communication is vital. It can be embarrassing—or worse—when key information doesn't get to the right people. That's why one pastor urged:

> "Never assume anything. Take the time to keep the right people in the loop. If you have to err between under and over-communicating, over-communicate. Every single time. Repeat yourself—remembering that most people don't listen carefully (and also they have to hear something about seven times before it registers). What seems obvious to you is probably not clear *at all* to others. Follow up oral interactions with written reviews of here's what we said.

> "A good question to ask about *everything* you send out—texts, emails, newsletters, social media posts, etc. is 'How might someone possibly misunderstand this?'"

Finances. Some pastors I interviewed said that financial concerns related to the church were a major source of organizational stress. One admitted, "For me, ministry pressure meant needing $100,000 every

Sunday to operate the ministry. If I felt pressure and stress, it was usually because of the finances we needed to run the church."

For another, financial pressures arose when he tried to give his youth pastor a much-needed, much-deserved raise. This desire precipitated a conflict with a major church donor:

> "I ran afoul of the church boss, the largest giver in the congregation. He probably gave twenty percent of the church income. We actually had a good relationship—I had led his brother to the Lord, and I'd helped his son come back to the Lord.
>
> "But when I tried to give our youth pastor a meager $800-a-year raise, this man didn't think that was the right thing to do. We actually got into an open conflict in a business meeting. He finally stood up and said, 'You're going to suffer. This church is *not* going to suffer!'"

That right there is the double whammy of organizational stress—a church business meeting *and* an argument over staff salaries! Yikes!

Thankfully, another pastor noted how situations like that—as stressful as they are—offer us a chance to see *what kind of leader we are*:

> "You don't find out what kind of leader you are in the good times. It's when the economy is going to pot and you got to deal with that. Or you're not meeting the budget and you have to cut expenses. *That's* when you find out what kind of leader you are, what kind of person you are, and what kind of fire you have in your soul. I learned to see organizational stress less as a negative and more as a positive."

QUESTIONS FOR REFLECTION / DISCUSSION

- What's your favorite oxymoron?

- Do you agree that issues of organization create a lot of stress for pastors?

- To repeat some of the questions raised in the chapter:

- Can the church itself—with all its activities and ministries—unwittingly contribute to the problem of pastoral burnout? In other words, do some structures make pastoral burnout more likely?

- How do we keep elaborate programs and complicated systems from becoming "larger than life" and the proverbial "tail that wags the dog"?

- How do pastors of growing churches avoid creating "organizational monsters" that chew them up and spit them out, even as they grind volunteers to the nubs?

- What if a church badly needs organization, but its pastor is bad at organization?

- What are your primary organizational stressors?

- What good but "not *necessary*" programs could you eliminate to make church less stressful for everyone?

- Is your church mission and vision clear?

- Do you have a clear job description? Do your staff members?

- Do you look forward to going to work most days?

CHAPTER 8

Occupational Hazards

If you've ever been part of a church plant (or a smaller church), your heart will go out to Damian. What a week he's had. Check this out:

On Sunday a.m. at the building where the congregation meets, a toilet in the ladies' room clogged and overflowed. Damian had to find a plunger and play the role of plumber, then custodian—woohoo!—for about 30 minutes right before the service. (Not the usual way preachers like to prepare their hearts!)

Immediately after the service, Mrs. Ezell, a godly, older woman in the congregation gave Damian a tongue-lashing for what he said in his message about the toilet incident. (He had tried to make some jokes about the "commode crisis"—and let's just say she did not find his humor humorous.)

Right after that, his volunteer kids' ministry leader pulled him aside to tell him "I just can't do this anymore" and that he needed to find someone else. Meanwhile six people—including two first-time visitors—left the building only to discover their cars had been towed during the service (they had unknowingly parked in spaces reserved for a nearby business).

Damian spent most of Sunday evening trying to smooth things out with the visitors. On Monday he was busy working out a parking agreement with the neighboring business owner and trying to find a new volunteer to lead the children's ministry.

Monday night, he got the call that Mrs. Ezell had suffered a massive, fatal heart attack! After consoling her sobbing son, the man asked Damian "Can you conduct her funeral on Friday?"

Tuesday, Damian spent most of the day chasing down other preachers to pick their brains about "how to do a funeral."

On Wednesday and Thursday, Damian engaged in a non-stop juggling act: Several counseling appointments, three lunch meetings (yep, in just two days), preaching prep, funeral prep, volunteer recruiting, talking to the director of the neighborhood Boys & Girls Club about a possible partnership, and . . . you get the drill.

Friday was the funeral, and Damian did a really good job. He got lots of positive comments, but, man was he tired when it was over!

Saturday, while Shondra took a day to get away by herself, Damian was halfway watching the kids, halfway watching the game, and halfway trying to wrap up his sermon.

And, boom, suddenly it was Sunday again!

Sound familiar?

THE JOB-RELATED STRESSORS OF MINISTERS

We've said this already, but it bears repeating: *Pastors have a lot of responsibilities and wear a lot of hats.* You're a mentor and a counselor, a preacher and a servant. You have to be ready at any moment to stop what you're doing and roll up your sleeves. Handyman? Chauffeur? Arbitrator? Errand boy? Sounding board? Newsletter writer/editor? Receptionist? You can never be sure what a day will hold.

All these job-related duties and emergencies can (and do) trigger stress. What are the most common ministerial stressors? We could *probably* mention three hundred; for brevity's sake, we'll mention just three.

1. Having too many responsibilities

After people/relational stressors, job-related stressors were the second dominant theme to emerge in my survey of pastors. More than a third of those I interviewed talked about the stress that arises from the multiple responsibilities on their shoulders. They described the intense pressure of trying to carry out the multiple facets of their job descriptions.

Remember the famous plaque that former U.S. President Harry S Truman kept on his Oval Office desk: "The buck stops here"? One pastor described the ministry as being like this. No matter the time of day or the day of the week, ultimate responsibility in a church lies with the senior pastor:

> "You have a staff to lead. You have administrative duties you've got to carry out. You've got sermons to preach. That doesn't take into consideration the phone call you get at three in the morning because one of your key leaders has been in a car wreck, or some member's wife left them, or some other emergency.

> "The President doesn't just serve Monday through Friday nine to five. The President takes an oath to serve as the nation's executive leader for the next four years. That's 24 hours a day, 365 days a year, for four years. Eight, if he or she gets re-elected.

> "It's like that for a pastor. I can go on vacation, but if one of my staff is in a crisis or someone has an automobile accident and it's a matter of life and death, I've got to drop everything and go. I'm the pastor. So, when you put all of those things together: you're the counselor, the shepherd, the chief fund-raiser, the primary spokesman for the church, you don't have to go looking for stress; stress comes looking for you!"

Other pastors talked about trying to prioritize their duties—so they could fulfill the essential ones and perhaps delegate the rest. But one pastor said even this act of prioritizing created stress:

> "Every day there are things I should have done and people I should have contacted. I can't do it all. I did all I could do today. I did the things I thought were most important and I'll do what I can tomorrow. I'm averaging a funeral a week. I've buried 1,500 people since I've been the pastor!

> "A pastor has to learn to go to bed every night knowing there are 100 things he didn't get done. Think about it. Think how many times he has a chance to screw up. I mean, he might, in a single weekend be called on to officiate a wedding, perform a funeral, conduct a baptism and preach several times."

Are we suggesting that being a pastor is more stressful than other jobs? Or that pastors experience nothing but stress all the time? The pastors I talked with didn't think so. Several acknowledged that stress was simply a function of their job; it was to be expected. One said:

> "You have to remember that ministry is a calling. And you have to constantly keep that in your heart as a pastor, realizing that you're leading people and you're leading an organization that supposedly serves those people. And whether it's the people that work with you, the leaders within your church, or the people in your fellowship, whether they are depleting your life or replenishing your life, that's a part of life and that's a part of ministry, and I think you have to accept that. And you have to walk in there each day and not always be thinking of stress."

Other pastors echoed these sentiments. One said, "Stress is just part of the job. I don't expect anything other than the pressure that I feel every night when I go to bed." Another concurred, saying, "I've always accepted that stress is just a part of what I do. It's kind of like if you can name the bear, the bear isn't so big and bad."

Still another added this sober warning: "I've been where a lot of guys are, and I sympathize and empathize with the pastors who are under stress. A lot of unfair and undue stress gets put on too many pastors. Under the best of circumstances, it's a stressful job… a lot of work."

Most of these older, veteran pastors came across as supremely confident in their interviews. Maybe that's because they've weathered the dark side of stressful seasons and reaped the rewards of endurance. But we cannot ignore the fact that some of these men came dangerously close to burning out and even to leaving the faith. As one put it:

> "Stress in ministry is a very real thing. It drove me out of the ministry at one point and I spent ten years running from God. It was because I did not know how to handle stress. My wife was young and naïve and she didn't know how to handle it either. We certainly didn't know how to talk about it. It was like the elephant in the room that both of us knew existed, but wouldn't acknowledge. Stress finally drove me to a place of literally taking my Bible and saying to God, 'You can take this and shove it, I'm through!' And I was. I walked away. And I figure that was at least ninety-nine percent stress-induced."

2. Preaching

For most pastors, preaching is *always* on their minds. You're reliving the message you just preached (and maybe cringing at what you said), or you're rolling around ideas for your next sermon. This obsession can be difficult to understand for anyone who doesn't preach weekly. Here's how one pastor described his pulpit experience:

> "I don't think people understand the stress of preaching. It's always right there. It's the kind of thing that, if you're passionate about it the way I am, it's always on your mind. I love it, but

I tell people it's like giving birth every Sunday and then, on Monday, finding out you're pregnant again!"

Another pastor used the same colorful "giving birth" analogy, adding:

"Now obviously we males have never given birth, but I've been with my wife when she did, and I tell people, 'As a bystander, you get the joy of *seeing* the baby; you don't have to endure the agonizing labor pains necessary to bring that baby into the world!' That's why, for me, preaching is the greatest stress week in, and week out. Sunday's coming. That means you've got to bring it again."

Multiple pastors agreed that the constant pressure of preaching new sermons each week was a constant burden. One pastor's response represents something I think we can all relate to: "Sundays are relentless. Ever since last Sunday ended, next Sunday has been coming... and that brings with it the unending challenge of sermon preparation. This is where I think that many pastors feel the stress the most. It never lets up."

And it's not just that the Sundays keep coming at you. According to another pastor: "It doesn't matter how great a message you preached last week, you'd better come back this weekend with another that is as good or better than last week's!"

No doubt, the preaching stress pastors feel is intensified by the fact that our people can listen 24/7 to phenomenally gifted preachers online. It's hard not to feel some pressure when you know you're being compared to Andy Stanley, Matt Chandler, David Platt, or John Piper.

One of the pastors I interviewed emphasized this reality:

"Preaching well is hard work. I teach our interns that. Sunday comes every seven days. For me, it's *the agony and the ecstasy*. Add to that the fact that we are being compared to other great teachers of the word. Our people are listening to all the finest preachers on their smartphones and computers. They want to know 'why can't you preach like that?'"

This makes sermon preparation all the more important. It ratchets up the pressure "to hit a preaching home run" every weekend. One pastor talked about this stress to perform: "My primary stressors deal with being excellent at preaching. The creative pressure of preaching to the same people for twenty-five years....The stress that comes in crafting new materials that are biblically solid and culturally relevant."

Said another: "On Sunday mornings, I am here at the office by 3:30 a.m. My message is all done, but I'm not. I'm not ready to get up and go. God still has to work on me."

One explained the high expectations he put on his own preaching this way: "The biggest pressure I feel every week is, *This is God's Word for God's people today.* I want to serve them well. That's the scary thing for me every week, and I never feel prepared. I never feel ready to preach."

And for some pastors, it's not enough to get *one* message together each week:

> "In my earliest years of ministry, I was preaching *three* times a week... Sunday morning, Sunday night, Wednesday night... You go from not preaching at all to doing three a week. Just the amount of time that it takes for each message is an overwhelming task right there."

This is why more and more churches are going to a team-teaching approach. They have two or even three "teaching pastors" who share the pulpit. One pastor on such a team said:

> "When we went to a team-teaching model (our most gifted preacher speaking twice a month, and two other pastors each preaching once a month), some of the members of our congregations were like, 'Wait...what is this? At my old church, the senior pastor preached, like, 50 times a year! Now it's a bunch of guys, a different face every week!'

"But after a while, most came to love the freshness, the different personalities and perspectives and styles. It's been a great
thing for our body and really healthy for our pastoral staff."

I can vouch for this myself. I know that not everyone has a church
culture where they can pull this off because of entrenched ideas of what
a pastor is supposed to do, but we went to the multiple-teacher approach
about seven years in. Most did not like it at first, but we did it out of neces-
sity because we had just planted a second campus and I needed to be at
both. As we got further into it, I saw the great benefits that it provided. It
took the focus off one individual. It allowed for a rest week every other week
for the teaching pastors so they could balance being shepherds and not just
teachers, and it challenged the people of the church to learn from different
people and thus, different teaching styles. Now, we have four teaching pastors and a strong community between each of them that impacts the way
we teach each week.

Here's a third job-related stress of ministry. We've mentioned it
already, but since it's so prevalent, we need to talk more about it.

3. Dealing With Criticism

Criticism can (and does) come from every side. Denominational heads.
Board members. Church members. The community. A frustrated spouse
or child ("You're *never* home!"). Even the voices in your own head can be
vicious, especially if you're a perfectionist ("You *suck* at your job!"). Some
days doesn't it feel like all you're doing is dodging arrows from the time
your eyes open until the time you drift off to sleep?

In one study of pastors (not the one I conducted), criticism was
almost *always* taken negatively. These pastors described criticism variously
as:

- "a negative evaluation"

- "a rebuke"

- "akin to fault-finding; it's telling someone they don't measure up"

- "usually a negative assault . . . often by someone without all the facts"
- "a personal attack"
- "a real blow to the ego"
- "an assault to our competence"
- "demoralizing."[17]

One pastor in this particular focus group seemed to speak for all the others by saying: "Criticism is a term that is always negative. There is no such thing as positive criticism."

The overarching perception among these pastors was that criticism was unfair and often hostile. It sparks emotions like anger, frustration, pain, irritation, and guilt. A steady stream of criticism leads to stress, burnout, and, in some cases, pastors leaving the ministry for good.

But here's what an older pastor I interviewed said about dealing with such negativity: "What do you need to stay in ministry? Do you need everyone's approval? Well, good Lord, Moses would've been out his first week!" Or, consider the sage counsel of another who said: "You can't take criticism and opposition personally. If you do, then you're going to be stressed out all the time."

This is why, as one pastor put it, pastors need tender hearts and thick skin. A fragile sense of self-esteem that depends on the admiration of others may be why some pastors struggle to accept feedback (even when it's constructive).

One pastor shared this helpful advice he received:

"Years ago when I was going through a difficult time, and a faction in the church wanted me out, I went and sought counsel from an older businessman in our church. He was prominent and successful, an entrepreneurial, consultant kind of guy. What he told me sticks with me to this day (probably because it kind of shocked me a little bit): 'Son, sometimes you just have to outlast the bastards.' And that's essentially what I did. They all moved on and I'm still here."

Another pastor put things more politely, but made the same point:

"I've learned I'm not responsible for how people treat me or respond to me. I'm responsible for how I treat and respond to them. God taught me that in my first church. I had a family that was the most negative family I've ever seen in my life. The husband and wife marked their son and daughter with the same critical attitude. Often when I preached on Sundays I realized I was trying to preach just to them. One Sunday morning, God made it so clear to me, that 'if they won't listen to Me, why in the world would I think *you* could change them?' That gave me the freedom to stop preaching at them and just start preaching the Word."

"Receiving criticism" isn't listed on any pastor's official job description. But it's part of every pastor's daily experience. It is often hurtful and usually stressful, but it doesn't have to lead to burnout. We can learn to process it healthily. More on that in a later chapter.

QUESTIONS FOR REFLECTION / DISCUSSION

- How would you summarize your role within the church where you serve? Only use 1-2 sentences.

- Have you experienced changes in your pastoral role as your church has changed in size?

- If you could talk to your "younger pastor self," what would you say to him?

- Do you agree or disagree with the pastor who said his stress was like that of the President?

- Are you on call at all hours of the day, either officially or unofficially?

- How do you personally decide which of your duties is essential? What are your strengths?

- Would you say being a pastor brings constant stress to your life? Is there one part of your job that creates more stress than others… if so, what?

- What pressures do you feel surrounding preaching weekly?

- Can you relate to the pastors who compared sermons to giving birth each week?

- What is the highest number of times you've ever preached in one week?

- Do you ever feel insecure about your preaching?

- Have you ever met a pastor who couldn't handle criticism?

CHAPTER 9

Family Ties

When it comes to stress and pastors' families, two things are true:

1. A minister's family can be negatively impacted by the stressors of "churchworld."

2. A spouse and/or kids can also be a source of stress to a pastor who's trying to shepherd a flock.

Let's look at each of those realities.

THE MINISTRY CAN TAKE A TOLL ON YOUR WIFE AND KIDS.

Fifteen of the twenty pastors I interviewed reported that they tried to protect their wives from stress, in part by not sharing their own stress or talking about "church problems." Five pastors felt that their spouses experienced specific stress just by being a pastor's wife. This is an example of "role stress," pressure that spills over from one's job into one's personal life.

Keeping work stress separate from family life is a type of psychological disengagement. Detaching from work during off-hours helps buffer against the negative effects of high-demand jobs. Conversely, a failure or refusal to psychologically detach (i.e., being preoccupied with work) heightens the risk of emotional exhaustion, regardless of the job's actual demands. A common complaint among pastors' spouses was that, emotionally, the church came first for their husbands.[18]

A pastor admitted, with pain in his voice:

"I know now that for a lot of years I screwed up by 'oversharing' with my wife. She was my sounding board, and I 'vented' often to her, because nobody can keep a secret like her. However, she is also a preacher's kid—and comes from a pretty dysfunctional church background. So there I was coming home lots of nights talking about the goofy thing this elder said, or the dumb thing that staff member did. And I realize now what a mistake that was. It was *not* good for her soul. She didn't need to know all that junk! I got issues off my chest. But I stuck it all *in her mind!*

"If I could tell a young pastor anything, it would be, 'Please. For the love of God—and the love of your wife—don't make that same mistake!'"

A pastor's intense work routine (whether you term it devotion, being driven, or work-a-holism) can also be a source of stress to his family. One pastor recounted how early in his career, he was constantly trying to introduce people to Christ and get them plugged into his church, long after regular work hours. He eventually recognized this pattern was creating undue stress for his wife. His experience suggests that a fierce dedication to evangelism, combined with an external pressure to see one's church grow, can be a hazard for new pastors and their families.

It's not just wives. Sometimes a minister's children can suffer unfairly because of their dad's calling. One pastor told of such an incident:

"Just before entering the fourth grade, my oldest son switched from a small private school to a public school. There he was ostracized and ridiculed for being a P.K. The other kids didn't physically bully him; they were just mean. They ignored him some days, and on other days they called him names. My wife and I didn't find out about all this till years later. Let's just say the experience *really* messed with his heart."

Many ministers' families also feel the financial pressure of not being able to do the things that their friends—even some of their church friends—are doing. Going on ski trips, or attending elite summer camps or private schools are often impossibilities. In the words of one pastor:

> "When my oldest was in the eighth grade, his class did one of those whirlwind four-day trips to Washington D.C. to tour all the historical sights. They flew, stayed in a nice hotel, the works. Because of my salary, there was no way we could afford the $1,800 price tag. So my son had to stay behind and sit with one other child in a glorified 'study hall' all week.

> "Looking back, I'm not sure if that experience was harder for him or for me. As a dad, you want to give your kids certain experiences and opportunities. But when you're pastoring a small church that can't afford to pay you much, that's not always possible. You can't shield them from things like that, and that's painful."

Those are just a few of the ways "the ministry" can inflict stress on pastors' families.

But the converse could also be true. At times it could seem that your wife and/or children can be the source of stress that inhibits your ability to preach, teach, and shepherd.

YOUR FAMILY CAN AFFECT YOUR MINISTRY EFFECTIVENESS.

A pastor has informed his secretary he needs to study and is not to be disturbed. You can imagine his frustration minutes later when she buzzes to tell him that he has a phone call.

"I thought I told you no interruptions!" the pastor snaps.

The secretary replies, "Yes sir, you did, but it's your wife." The pastor thinks to himself, *This better be important. She knows this is my study time and I need to be able to focus.*

He takes the call, "What on earth is going on? Is there a crisis? This is my study time, and I don't like being interrupted."

His wife says, "Dear, you know I wouldn't disturb you unless it's *really* important. I just wanted to tell you about a marriage in the church that's falling apart."

Immediately the pastor's tone softens. With great compassion, he says, "Oh, that is important. Thank you for letting me know! Whose marriage are you talking about?"

There's a brief pause. Then the wife says flatly, "Yours."

Ouch.

When a minister's wife is struggling (whether spiritually, emotionally, relationally, etc.) it can't help but affect him. (Put it this way: If a pastor goes about the work of the ministry, *unaffected* by his bride's struggles, we have an even bigger problem!)

The reasons for an unhappy minister's wife can be many. (Note: Her struggles do *not* automatically suggest she's "unspiritual" or "rebellious." She may be dealing with personal baggage, or wrestling with her own faith, or, as Paul puts in in Philippians 2, "working out her salvation").

One pastor talked about the deep faith crisis his wife went through about 10 years into his ministry at his first church:

"All her troubling questions about God and the Bible that she'd been shoving down her whole life suddenly erupted like a volcano. She couldn't pretend anymore. Thankfully, she found some safe people and accepting environments where she could process openly and honestly. I tried to give her space and grace. That was a dark and scary time—for her and for me. But she emerged—with a more authentic faith and great compassion for those who struggle with doubt. Now her favorite verse is that great little prayer in Mark 9:24—'I do believe; help my unbelief.'"

Some pastor's wives get leery and/or weary of being in the proverbial fishbowl or placed on a kind of spiritual pedestal (choose your metaphor). This is what's going on with Damian's wife Shondra. As people flock to City Church and look to Damian at all hours for wisdom and counsel, she worries that people might expect the same from her—and she doesn't feel qualified to be in that position.

Other pastor's wives don't just fear unfair expectations that others in the church *might* place on them—they actually face them regularly. Still others feel lonely and isolated (for many pastor's wives, it's difficult to find trustworthy friends they can confide in). If a pastor's wife lives far from her family or the deep friendships she cultivated in a prior church, she may be grieving those losses.

How do you understand a wife's "less than enthusiastic" attitude toward ministry? Ask. Listen. Have honest conversations. We'll revisit this in the latter part of this book.

When a pastor's kids are struggling, it can't help but weigh on his heart. If you've got a child with a medical condition, or a learning disability, you know all about this.

If your son or daughter is acting out, or can't seem to make friends (or make the right kind of friends)...if your teens are becoming cynical about the faith, you know how distracted and anguished you can get. It's hard to sleep or focus.

A wise pastor once said, "Ministry should always begin in the home. Your family, not your congregation, should get your best attention, energy, and devotion."

Another said, "No amount of success in ministry can compensate for failure at home."

But—father alert—be extremely careful. It's easy to be physically present with your kids, but not mentally present. I remember when my kids were young, they would always get my attention by saying, "Daddy, Daddy, Daddy…" I think they understood somehow that it took calling me three times to get me to be present because my mind was often far away.

If your home is reeling from the stressors of ministry…or if it's a source of stress upon your ministry…maybe that's a divine wake-up call?

I just know you need to address it—and fast. You need a plan.

That's what we'll work on in the second half of this book.

QUESTIONS FOR REFLECTION / DISCUSSION

- Can you relate to how the pastors mentioned in this chapter tried to shield their wives from ministry stress? Why or why not?

- Do your church members treat or view your wife as an "unofficial church staff member"?

- Have your wife and kids been held to a higher standard by the church you serve?

- Have your wife and children ever been scapegoated/made to suffer for ministry decisions you made?

- In what specific ways has your family been impacted by ministry stress?

- How can a pastor keep his wife and kids from becoming bitter at the church?

- Have you ever shared information with your spouse that you wish you hadn't?

- If your children are grown, are they still involved in church? What would they say about their experience of growing up as "PKs"?

- What boundaries do you have in place to protect your family from the stress of ministry?

A **PLAN** FOR PASTORAL STRESS (SO YOU **DON'T** BURNOUT)

CHAPTER 10

Eliminating Unnecessary Stress

A guy walks into the ER late one Saturday night and moans, "Hey, Doc, I'm pretty sure I broke my arm in two places! What do you recommend?"

The doctor thinks for a moment and says, "Don't ever go back in those places!"

It's an old, corny joke, but also a great reminder. Some of the stress in our lives *is* avoidable. We don't have to sit around wishing certain problems would magically go away. Deliverance doesn't always require a miracle, or the stars lining up just so.

Sometimes a better life simply requires us to have courage and take action.

Remember: We have agency (i.e., the freedom to make choices). We have it within us to resolve a lot of the issues we face. We're not victims (not always, anyway). Just because we can't eliminate *every* stressful thing in our lives doesn't mean we can't get rid of some needless pressures.

In this chapter, we want to explore how to put some stressors in our rearview mirrors.

WHERE TO START?

Hear me. I'm *not* suggesting we can eliminate all our stress. Some hard things are unavoidable because, well, we live in a broken world full of broken people. And it's important to keep in mind that some stress is actually good for us. It motivates us to take needed action. What's more, God uses it to shape us into better versions of ourselves, which is the process of looking more like Him.

What I *am* saying is that stress takes a toll. If you tolerate avoidable stress or mishandle unavoidable stress, it will make you miserable. That's why it's vital to learn how to: (a) identify stress; (b) get rid of any and all avoidable pressures, and (c) learn how to cope with unavoidable strains in life.

We'll talk about how to cope with inescapable pressures later. For now, let's focus on identifying and eliminating needless stressors.

IDENTIFYING YOUR STRESSORS

The first step in responding to stress is simply to be aware of it. You have to get better at noticing things. You have to recognize what's going on both in and around you.

Several pastors reiterated the truth that "everybody responds and reacts to being tired or stressed a little differently." They also noted some clear behavioral and/or emotional signs that indicated that they were presently experiencing the presence and effects of stress:

- "I begin to get short with people. I have to watch myself for that."

- "My sleep starts getting restless."

- "When I find myself angry about little things, it's time to ask 'What is *that* about?'"

- "When I wake up and don't want to go to church or don't want to go preach… then I realize there's a problem. That's a bad place to get to."

- "I have a tendency to create a worst-case scenario—*and if this happens, then what am I going to do?* Silly, right? Getting stressed out about things that are highly unlikely to ever come about."

- "When I get stressed out, I start micromanaging everything—down to what the custodian was doing and how they were dusting."

One pastor I talked with admitted:

"My response to stress is often different. Sometimes when I feel a great deal of stress it makes me run to the Lord. I find myself saying, 'God, I can't do this on my own, I'm in way over my head.'

"There are other times when, almost like Jonah, I just want to get away from everything and everybody, even God! I've learned there's a big difference between being tired *of* the ministry and being tired *in* the ministry. It's okay to get tired *in* it, but I have to fight against getting tired *of* it because this is my calling."

What's the skill we need? *Awareness.* Pay attention to your body so that you can tell when the stress is starting to get to you. Take stock of your behaviors and thoughts. Notice any negativity you're feeling. Another pastor observed:

"When I'm stressed I get noticeably quiet and contemplative. Sometimes I become critical of my own heart and lose strength and confidence. But when I catch myself doing this, I see it as an invitation to press deeper into God. I have to widen my perspective. For instance, I may think what I'm going through is really bad, but God is saying, 'No, I can use this situation to develop something really good in you.'"

Perhaps as you read this, you're thinking, *How would I know if I'm feeling stressed? I'm not an introspective or touchy-feely guy.*

Trust me, self-awareness isn't a superpower that only a few get to enjoy. In a study of more than 350 Methodist pastors, the respondents who identified themselves as "burned out" were more than thirty times more likely to score in the high range for emotional exhaustion and sixteen times more likely to meet the criteria for being highly stressed.[19] In other words, they knew they were in trouble.

You may not always *want* to identify the stress in your life, but it's not because you *can't*.

One warning: Trying to identify and "name" your stress can have a dark side. It's possible to obsess over the pressures of ministry. This may be why one pastor I talked with noted, "I try not to really pay *too much attention* to stress because I think if you focus on it excessively, it gets worse."

In short, be observant. Practice awareness. Be healthily self-aware, without becoming self-absorbed.

Step one is *identifying* the stressors you're experiencing. Step two is ...

ELIMINATING THE STRESSORS YOU CAN CONTROL

Some stressors are unavoidable. If, as a senior pastor, it's been decided that you've got to preach 42 Sundays a year, then you've got to preach 42 Sundays. That's a non-negotiable. However, you *don't* have to make that part of your life even more stressful by waiting till Saturday afternoon to start prepping your sermon.

The point is you have the power to make some decisions—and changes—this week that can un-complicate your life. Let me just list ten.

1. **Take a hard look at your schedule.** If you're disorganized like Damian, the young pastor of City Church… if you don't have a clue where your time goes, try this. Track your activities for the next week or two. Actually keep a written log of everything you do.

   As you note all the ways you're spending your time, use a +10 to -10 scale to indicate your satisfaction/stress level while doing each activity. If visiting newcomers really energizes you and brings you joy, assign it an appropriate positive number. If sitting in long, tedious finance committee meetings makes you crazy, give that item a fitting negative number.

   When you're done, you'll have a good 30,000-foot view of how you're using your time and how each of those activities either blesses or stressors you.

2. **Have a gut-level talk with your wife and your board.** Show them your time-tracker. Ask them, "What things do *you* see me doing on a daily/weekly basis that are obviously frustrating to me…either because I'm not good at those things or I'm not adequately trained to do them?" Give them permission to speak freely and honestly. Try not to get defensive.

3. **Examine your expectations.** We all create expectations (usually unconsciously) about almost everything in life. And when reality doesn't measure up to what we expected, we feel disappointed.

   What are your expectations for your ministry? Your church? Your staff? Your kids? Your self?

   It's wonderful to be optimistic, and it's commendable to trust God. But the *goals* for your ministry and life need to be realistic. A pastor who lives in a rural community of twelve hundred probably shouldn't *expect* his church to grow to a thousand members in three years. (If he does, he's almost surely setting himself up for major disappointment—and lots of unnecessary stress.) Remember, there's a world of difference between *desiring* certain things and *demanding* them. Demanding people are seldom joyful.

4. **Check your heart for control issues.** When it gets right down to it, a minister has control over very little. Oh, you can do your part as a faithful pastor. You can pray diligently and trust deeply and love others well. You can study and preach and serve.

However, you *can't* change a life or save a soul or rescue a marriage. Those are things only God can do. *He* is in charge of outcomes—not you! We don't get to play the role of the Holy Spirit in people's lives. The quicker a pastor comes to terms with this humbling, but freeing truth, the less stressful and more enjoyable his ministry will be. Said one pastor, "It is not the preacher's job to fill the pews. His job is to fill the pulpit. Don't get that confused. Preach the Word. Leave the results to God."

Delegate some things. Remember Exodus 18? The fascinating story of Jethro watching Moses spend an entire day trying to settle the petty arguments of a long line of unhappy Israelites? Jethro straight up told his stretched-thin son-in-law, "What you are doing is not good." He warned him, in so many words that he was headed for burnout! Then he urged him to delegate the bulk of this overwhelming responsibility to others. Thank God Moses listened. Delegation is ingenious. It's a godsend!

Six pastors I spoke with pointed to the art of delegation as a helpful way of eliminating their stress.

One said, "I am not a pastoral counselor... I've always had a real clear understanding that I do basically four things: preaching, teaching, leadership, and evangelism. I let my staffers do the rest."

Another said, "The key to delegating, and where a lot of guys make mistakes, is this: We can't delegate responsibility without delegating authority. With that being said, don't delegate anything until you can trust the person you're delegating to. I never, ever try to do anything that somebody else can do for me because I need to be doing what only I can do. And that's primarily casting a vision, providing leadership, and preparing to preach the Word."

Yet another agreed, noting that it would be a near-impossible feat to be everywhere his presence is requested: "My people want me to do every funeral and wedding and respond to every crisis, and I don't. I can't be the Superman pastor for everybody."

For many, the real issue was *letting go of control*:

> "In the beginning, I had more difficulty letting things go because this church was a baby that I had helped birth. Letting go wasn't easy for me. Besides, in my mind, I thought no one could do things as well as I could. I had pretty high standards. Some would call that being a perfectionist, being anal, being whatever."

> "It became easier as the years went on, mostly out of necessity. I got more comfortable about not having to know everything. I was able to trust in good, effective staff and leaders. Some of them even got to where they thought I didn't care, but it wasn't that at all. It was simply an evolution, a maturing on my part of where I didn't really have to have my hand on everything."

Surely, the ideal is to be surrounded by skilled people. The best-case scenario is to be able to say, as one pastor did, "I never take myself too seriously. Part of the reason is that, well, I really can't, because I'm always around people who are way smarter than I am... I'm just lucky to serve... you know?"

But there is still a need for caution. Delegation itself can bring stress, as it did for this pastor: "My stress is giving away ministry when I want to do it myself. But one of the things I've learned to do is to trust the godly men that God has placed around me."

This is a hard lesson, but one worth learning *early*.

In short, wise leaders recognize where they're *not* gifted—and where they are *most* gifted. They do what they do best and gladly let others use their gifts for God's glory.

5. **Stop reading angry, anonymous notes.** Tell your congregation, "You can send us a note about ANYTHING. You can tell us what you don't like. You can offer any honest feedback; however, if your note isn't signed, it's going straight into the trashcan. We won't bother reading it. We're glad to discuss any issue, but we will not be your dartboard." Anonymous criticism is cowardly. Why add that unnecessary stress to your life?

6. **Learn the word "no"** (and its related phrase, "I'm sorry, I can't!"). Nobody likes to let others down; however, if you try to be a people pleaser, the ministry will kill you. If you do find that you are a pushover and quick to let people guilt you into things, try this. Say "no" to at least one request a day, for a whole week. Then evaluate the results.

7. **Ask for/get a clearer job description.** If your pastoral role is ill-defined, if there are things you *think* your board expects from you, but you're not *sure*, ask. You may be stressed in part because you're doing things no one ever asked you to do! With your staff, make a list of all the duties that need to be performed around your church. If there are important duties no one is currently doing, and you are tempted to take them on, see item #5.

8. **Shut down something**. Are there programs or ongoing activities at your church that are overextending you, putting stress on your staff, and wearing out your people? Why not put one or two of them out of its (and out of *your*) misery? Stop feeding the monster!

   I call this "Leaving the 'dropped ball' alone." Inevitably in ministry, a staff member or volunteer will "drop a ball." Instinctively, we want the ball picked back up, but I say, wait. Watch. See if anybody else picks it up first. If someone grabs it, more than likely, it is something they are passionate about. If nobody picks it up, maybe it's something that has served its purpose and now needs to be put to rest.

   Here's a radical example: Where is it written down: "Thou shalt have a Sunday night preaching and worship service (after you've already had a good one on Sunday morning)"? If that evening meeting is poorly attended, and if it's something that feels to everyone more like a "have to" than a "get to," why keep doing it? Why not allocate that time and staff energy for something else that will help you better fulfill your mission?

   (NOTE: If you do this, you will—at least temporarily—have the stress of people lamenting, "But we've ALWAYS had a _____." They will get over it. And besides, many of them will be people who didn't participate in the event anyway.)

9. **Don't put up with problem volunteers or staff.** If you've got a board member who's giving you fits, you can't exactly fire him. You're probably stuck. But a *staff member* or *volunteer* who's more trouble than he or she is worth? That's a different story.

   As one pastor said, "Sometimes we think we're being very gracious to allow staff members to stay when they just don't fit. But in fact, we're being gracious when we send them on because that is better for everyone. If we are not honest about this, we are just wasting their time and inviting unnecessary tension."

Another said, "I had a volunteer once who tried to hijack our small group ministry. (He was actually a very gifted guy. In fact, he had been the small group pastor at his previous church.) We gave him an inch of authority and he tried to take the proverbial mile. Suddenly, he was trying to drag us in a direction we didn't want to go. And his 'know-it-all' personality didn't help things. When he balked at our attempts to rein him in, I had no choice but to 'un-volunteer' him. He left the church angry. To me, it was what I like to call 'a blessed subtraction.'"

Speaking of "firing" people reminds me that we probably need to talk about...

MAKING HARD DECISIONS

When you're stressed, making decisions often feels monumental. However, some decisions, even hard ones can make your life more peaceful. Here is one pastor's experience when his church experienced explosive growth:

"As the church grew, the price I paid was significant. It meant I would not personally know everyone who became a part of our congregation. But I really had no choice; you have to develop staff and you have to let go of things you love holding onto. It wasn't that I felt I reached out to new people better than anybody else. It's just that I was having to give up something I really loved."

This doesn't come naturally to every pastor, but it is necessary if a church is going to grow to thousands of members. Not that this is the goal of every church. My point is that greater size requires the hard decision to delegate. Here is what another of the pastors said in his interview:

> "I never wanted to build buildings. I just wanted to reach people. But after we started reaching people, we needed a place to put them. That caused me a lot of stress. As a church grows you can't wear all the hats anymore. You have to give some of them up. As John Maxwell says, 'If you have to have your hand on everything, the church will never move beyond your reach.'"

Growth does create new problems, but it can also be a safeguard against other stressors. One pastor noted:

> "When you have new people coming in all the time the old people can't say, 'Preacher, if you don't do this or that, we're going to take our group and go find another church.' Because we're steadily growing, I always have the luxury of saying, 'We'll be praying for you!' Growth keeps those power cells from developing."

Almost every father can recall a child saying something like, "Daddy, when I press my arm right here, it really hurts."

The standard Dad response? (Should we say it in unison?) "Well, stop pressing your arm right there!"

The point is there *are* things we can do to eliminate certain stressors *altogether*. When so much pastoral pressure is inescapable, doesn't it make sense to get rid of any and every stress that we can avoid?

QUESTIONS FOR REFLECTION / DISCUSSION

- What's your top takeaway from this chapter?

- What are some avoidable stressors you've been putting up with and why do you think that you put up with them?

- What could you eliminate from your schedule? What programs could you cut?

- Do you find it hard to say "no"? Why?

- How much do "unrealistic expectations" add to your stress load?

- How good (or how willing) are you when it comes to delegation?

CHAPTER 11
How 'bout Some "R & R"?

On Tuesday, Pastor Ken trudges into the house at 6:15 p.m. (He's been up at the church since leaving for an elder meeting at 5:35 a.m.)

His wife takes one look and says, "Bad day?"

"Eh. It was fine. That is until Bob came by this afternoon." (Bob, for the record, is a retired truck driver, proud Navy veteran, and active church member. Bob's a nice guy, but he can be socially awkward.)

"Oh, no. What did Bob do now?"

"He didn't *do* anything. It's what he keeps *saying*. Every time he sees me now, he goes out of his way to say 'What an easy job! Ha, ha. You preacher guys only work one hour a week.' No kidding, if I had a dollar for every time he's made that crack this year, I could take you out to dinner—a nice dinner—right now. The thing is he says it like he's joking. But there's also this little edge in his voice."

"Yeah, well, that's ridiculous. I wouldn't give that another thought. Maybe if he'd said you only *rest* an hour a week."

Ken responds, quite sanctimoniously, "Wait. What do you mean?! *I rest!*"

Tracy looks up from the stove, incredulous. "Uh, really? And when exactly do you do that? You mean the five to six hours' sleep you get every night? Ken, you haven't really *rested* since you got out of college."

∗ ∗ ∗ ∗

WHY IS RESTING SO DIFFICULT FOR SO MANY PASTORS?

Whether it's due to an urgent passion to introduce people to Christ and help them grow in the faith...or because of workaholic tendencies, the Savior Complex, a sense of false guilt, a bad habit of people-pleasing, etc., many pastors have a hard time going "off duty" and resting.

We can't create a plan for dealing with pastoral stress without talking about this need for pastoral rest.

REST IS MANDATORY, NOT OPTIONAL.

When you think about it, rhythm is what makes music good. Rhythm is not just about when to play, but also, when NOT to play an instrument or a note.

Life is like music. For it to be good, it needs a rhythm—activity followed by inactivity (or rest). This can be seen as early as Genesis 1. In the creation narrative, there is a rhythm that you can sense, "there was evening and morning, the first day... the second day... all the way to the sixth day. But then something striking happens. God rests on the seventh day and all of a sudden there is no mention of, "there was evening and morning." The seventh day is a rest to the rhythm of the rest of the week.

The Scriptures highly exalt both the idea and the practice of *rest*. According to the creation account in Genesis, God rested after creating the world . . . but *not* because he was pooped out. Instead, he paused to enjoy what he'd done the previous six days.

Exodus 31:17 even notes that the Almighty was "refreshed" by this "day off."

And I think it's very important to recognize that man was created on the sixth day and then came the seventh. In other words, the very first thing that Adam did was rest! God didn't start him off with a to-do list or a bunch of chores. He didn't immediately have him start planting fields, or reap a harvest or even name the animals. No, the FIRST thing Adam did was rest with God and appreciate and admire! In other words, rest is a top priority with God!

This means if we want to be godly, we need to learn how to rest. If we want to be imitators of God (Ephesians 5:1), we need to go off duty for *at least* one day out of every seven.

Long before there were any nations or religious systems, God built this kind of work-rest rhythm into the very fabric of creation. This is why crops die. Fruit trees drop their leaves and stop being productive for a season. Animals hibernate.

Later, when the tribes of Israel became a nation at Mount Sinai, God built this important requirement for rest right into their calendar. Each week, they were to take a day off. No "doing" just a whole lot of "being." In addition, God stipulated additional, extended times of rest—joyous festivals that extended for days. There were whole years (every seventh one, to be specific) in which farmers weren't even supposed to plant crops! For the ancient Israelites, resting was serious business!

And it was needed! Think about it. Before receiving the Law that mandated a Sabbath rest for them, they were previously slaves in Egypt. There they had been forced to make bricks every day. No days off. No vacations. And this was their life for well over 400 years!

In essence, their value was determined by how many bricks they could make. God had a better idea. He wanted them to take a day a week to undo what the other six days did to them. They needed to take one day a week and disconnect completely from work. This was to remind them "You are not machines. Your worth is not gauged by how much you produce.

Your worth comes from the fact that I, your God, have chosen you, freed you, and made you my own. That is where your value comes from."

Later, when God stepped out of eternity into time in the person of Jesus, he made resting a top priority and regular practice. Like every faithful Jew, he observed the Sabbath. Once when he was worn out during a boat ride, he grabbed a cushion and grabbed forty winks (see Mark 4:38). Who knew naps were "spiritual"? Another time, when Jesus sensed his followers were weary after a rigorous "mission trip," he declared a retreat to a secluded place where they could "rest a while" (Mark 6:31, nasb).

Rest isn't a sign of weakness. And it isn't a dereliction of your pastoral duties. Rest is vital.

The pastor who works 70 hours a week doesn't deserve our praise. He deserves our pity. If he burns out, he won't be able to help anyone.

WHAT DOES PASTORAL "R & R" (REST AND REFRESHMENT) LOOK LIKE?

Here are some simple ways to cultivate the critical habit of rest into your busy ministry life:

Take a day off.
Question: Do you take a day off? I'm not getting into the argument about the actual day of the week (that is for another book at another time). I am more interested in the point of the "quality of time" that you spend every week. Do you take a day a week to undo what the other six days did to you?

Question: If and when you *do* take a "day off," are you really "off"? Do you fully disconnect from all the pressures of your job? Because—news flash—if you keep your phone next to you and spend your "day off" responding to church-related texts and emails . . . or if you spend it reading a book that's about ministry or preaching better, etc., you're not really "off." You're still working. You're just not working *at the office.*

For the love of God—and as a step of faith—unplug! Stop tending to people. God's big enough to care for them. You're important, but you're not *that* necessary. Believe it or not, your church won't implode if you go off duty. (Although you might if you don't). Don't forget, the Church is not your bride. She belongs to Christ! Don't get caught up in an affair with the bride of Christ!

Take a day a week to just be. Sit. Breathe. Notice. Count your blessings. Eat. Laugh. Doze. Take a walk. Read something fun—a good novel, a stirring biography, something off the bestseller list (that your people are probably reading).

I know. When you're a driven person, a day off seems impossible. You can't stop thinking about all the productive things you could be doing.

It's hard to think of an hour apart from what that hour can produce. Have you ever caught yourself saying something like, "I just wasted a whole hour on that"? Or can you remember the last time you said, "Where did this day go?" We often find ourselves just going and going and going. And still, there is not enough time to get everything done. These become the thoughts that keep us awake at night creating that internal anxiety.

The idea of stopping and resting might make you feel, as one country preacher put it, "as jittery as a long-tailed cat in a room full of rocking chairs." That's okay. Do it anyway. You'll get better at resting in time. It takes practice. Just know you don't *always* have to be productive. Your worth isn't connected to your accomplishments.

One pastor said that scheduling a day off during the week should be imperative. And another day should offer you the chance to be spontaneous. "I always encourage young pastors when I'm trying to speak into their lives, to make one of the days they work a day they can call 'audibles.' I think the problem is so often guys just don't... I know now I can give up a Friday if I want. That's my choice."

Take a vacation.

One pastor said that scheduling a vacation every six months was crucial for recharging from the stress of his job.

Another pastor's wife plans shorter trips—quarterly getaways—to "get out of Dodge" and revitalize—even if it's just a long, three-day weekend. Still another described these sorts of getaways as mental incentives for when stress is especially strong:

> "My wife now plans a little trip about once a quarter because that keeps me fresh and helps me to recover. When you're under the gun for so long, you start to get tired. I'm tired right now, but I know I've got some days coming up on the calendar where I'm going to slip away. I'll be able to sleep in, sit there and read, see some sites, eat some good food, unwind, do whatever. And that helps me say mentally, 'Hang on. Don't jump on this person over here. You're going to be too harsh. When you start to correct them, you're going to over-correct. Wait. A time of rest is just ahead.'

Maybe this is why Jesus told his disciples to "come apart and rest" (Mark 6:31). Without such "rest," we might just come apart!

A lack of rest typically leads to a lack of perspective. When we are caught up in the chronic stress of ministry it seems that we cannot see beyond it. When this happens, we become convinced that things are always going to be like this… "These people will never listen." "No one likes my vision for this church." "This staff is lazy." "This community is so uninterested in spiritual things."

Once this thinking sets in, we become more convinced that this "place" is not a good fit for us, and we begin to look to move somewhere else that might be a better fit. Or worse, we entertain the thought of leaving ministry altogether.

However, one thing that was consistent with every one of these pastors that I interviewed was their perspective on difficult times (and great times for that matter). They adopted the perspective that "Things won't always be like this." It's true. How many times did you walk through a difficult time in your life only to look back and think, "Why was I so concerned about that?"

Let me offer an illustration. Envision this scenario: You're suddenly been called on to take care of someone else. Because of the person's life situation, they can't do anything for themselves. You have to feed them, clothe them, bathe them, drop everything whenever they cry for help. There is not a minute of the day when you can leave them by themselves.

Sound depressing? Feeling trapped? Okay . . . but what if I told you that person is an infant?

Not so depressing anymore, right?!? Why? Because you know your situation won't always be this way. That's the power of perspective... and the same is true of ministry.

Take up a hobby.
One study found that pastors who are resilient are that way, at least in part, because they've learned to emotionally and physically disengage from the demands of their ministry and rejuvenate themselves. They're good at setting boundaries and they spend time doing worthwhile things. The rural pastors surveyed seemed to lack this ability, even with access to a variety of formal and informal supports.[20]

In other words, pastors need hobbies. You need a way to burn off stress: running, hunting, painting, cycling. Of course, you have to pick activities carefully. You need *recreation* that fosters a kind of *re-creation* (i.e., it brings order and stability to your frazzled, chaotic soul). You want activities that help you cope with your stress. If a hobby like golf or fishing frustrates you more than it re-energizes you, find a different hobby. Seek out activities that bring *balance* and *variety* and *joy* to your life.

Have you got a hobby? If not, get one! Pastor, you are no less a man of God when you are fishing, ballroom dancing with your wife, or even cooking than you are when you're reading a book on systematic theology or writing a sermon. You need creative outlets and restorative endeavors to fill your tank. That's the only way to thrive when you are neck-deep in doing life with your flock.

Take a sabbatical.

A sabbatical is an extended time away from ministry every seven years (or so). Most are usually from six *weeks* to six *months* in duration. The goal of such a break isn't to become a couch potato; it is to restore your soul. A sabbatical isn't the same thing as a vacation (although a vacation may start or conclude a sabbatical).

A good sabbatical should include time for rest, reflection, recreation, perhaps counseling or even taking a course or getting specialized training. A wise, well-planned break results in a pastor who is refreshed and re-energized. He has clearer vision, renewed passion, and a fresh perspective. He's rested and raring to resume the work of shepherding a flock.

The sabbatical idea is awesome in theory (and usually in practice). Still, it's tricky. In some churches—usually smaller and/or independent churches—the idea of pastoral sabbaticals can create conflict. The notion is often dead on arrival. All too often board members (and church members) are quick to protest, "Two months off?! Gimme a break! My employer doesn't give *me* a sabbatical! And my job is just as stressful as *his*!"

Also, the logistics of taking time away can be tough to work out, as one pastor discovered:

> "In the 24 years I served at my last church, I was given two sabbaticals, each one six weeks in length. In the first instance, I was given no instructions about how to make the most of that time off. There was no plan, and I had no clue what to do with myself. I read some, tried (in vain) to sleep in. I discovered it's hard to 'withdraw' in a small town. If I left the house, I'd see church people, and it was tough to not feel like I was still on duty. Mostly I puttered around for six weeks, feeling restless. I

was thankful for the break, but I felt like I wasn't really taking advantage of it. It kinda felt like 'house arrest.'

"My second sabbatical came right after our church merged with another congregation. That whole merger process was good, but it was also exhausting. And yet I didn't feel I should leave town and get a change of scenery for two reasons: One, many of the folks in our body were freaked out by all the changes—both real and imagined. And, two, my son was a senior in high school. So I tried to stay put, and it was hard to create new restorative routines.

"If I were going to grade myself in 'Taking Sabbaticals 101,' I'd give myself a D at best. I could have used a lot more guidance. In hindsight, I wish I'd talked to older pastors about what to do."

You may think to yourself, "Great advice! I'm all for it! But, simply put, there is no way my church is going to let me take a sabbatical." I hear you. Not everyone understands the life of a pastor, therefore not everyone understands the need, let alone the value, of a sabbatical.

This is where you have to do your work. I have found that, although hesitant at first, most churches are very generous with time for a sabbatical when they understand exactly what it is. You should begin now to educate your church.

Help them understand that a sabbatical is not "time off;" it is a redirection of priorities for a time. Help them grasp that when you focus on growing yourself, it directly benefits them. Help them picture what happens on a sabbatical. Give them examples of what a pastor does on a sabbatical (e.g., reading, learning, studying, engaging with other leaders and mentors).

Next, begin to tell them that you "plan to" or "look forward to" taking some time to grow yourself. Start talking about it now so they will have time to get used to the idea.

Finally, have a plan. Who will speak for you when you are out? What will you do on sabbatical? When will you return? You will find that when your church understands what you will be doing, they will be more accepting of the idea.

Take a nap.
You might be one of those people who *can't* nap—at least not without it messing up your sleep cycle at night, or making you feel groggy the rest of the day. But it might be that a short, 15-minute "power nap" in the afternoon could be re-energizing for you.

The point? Closing your eyes and nodding off for 30 minutes or 8 hours isn't unspiritual. It doesn't mean you're weak or lazy. It means you're human. As we've already mentioned, Jesus napped. And we saw how the Old Testament prophet Elijah was exhausted after doing spiritual battle on Mount Carmel with the prophets of Baal. The divine prescription? God fed him a meal and put him down for some much-needed sleep.

In one sense, napping and/or sleeping is a great sign of faith. It's essentially saying to God, "I can't keep going. I'm temporarily out of gas. But because I know you watch over me and never slumber or sleep, I can go 'off-duty' and trust you with all my concerns."

In the great words of the psalmist, "I lie down and sleep; I wake again, because the Lord sustains me" (Psalm 3:5)

Just to repeat and say "Amen!" to what one pastor said, "Sometimes the most spiritual thing you can do is take a nap."

QUESTIONS FOR REFLECTION / DISCUSSION

- What grade would you give yourself when it comes to obeying the biblical commands to rest?

- What grade would your wife give you?

- Talk about your day off—what you do (or why you don't take a day off).

- What is vacation like for you? What would be your ultimate vacation?

- Is it hard for you to unplug when you take a day off or leave town for vacation?

- Have you ever taken a Sabbatical? If so, what was that experience like?

- What would your board or congregation say if you asked for a Sabbatical?

- What counsel would you give to a pastor embarking on his first sabbatical?

- Are you a napper? Why or why not?

CHAPTER 12
The Power of Healthy Relationships

Brother Charles did something last weekend he hasn't done in at least five years. He got together with a group of old college buddies for what they call "The Festival of Meat."

Back in the day, these seven were all knuckleheads together in a campus ministry at the state university. Now Charles and one other guy in the group are pastors. Three are attorneys. The other two are businessmen.

"The Festival of Meat" is a spectacle. The men meet up (or "meat up," I should say) in a central location for a weekend. They eat steaks and ribs and burgers. On Friday night they stay up and catch up. Exhausted, they swear they're going to sleep in the next morning. But of course, by 5:15 a.m. on Saturday, they've all had two big cups of coffee (at least). All day they're at it again, telling old stories and new ones, laughing at each other's quirks and foibles till they can't breathe.

Driving home, Brother Charles felt happier. Lighter. Suddenly, his ministry pressures didn't seem so overwhelming.

Why do you suppose?

* * * * *

There's a reason the Bible talks so much about relationships and friendships.

The fact is God made us for community. He wired us to need other people. Don't believe it? Look at how weird some people got during the COVID pandemic lockdown!

Relationships are everything. The Bible shows us that. Experience reiterates it. Friendship with God and deep connections with others are what make life worth living. Relationships also make life bearable. Who was the Swedish person who observed, "Shared joy is double joy; shared sorrow is half sorrow"? (That person was a genius.)

But of course, you can't share joy and sorrow unless you have people in your life to share such things with.

In this chapter, I want to reveal what pastors told me (and what I've experienced) about the power of relationships to keep us sane, grounded, and better able to deal with the stressors of life.

We'll look briefly at five kinds of relationships that pastors should consider: friends, peers/colleagues, confidants, mentors/mentees, and counselors.

1. Friends

I think we know why Brother Charles came home Sunday from his "Festival of Meat" in a much better frame of mind. He experienced what the late, great C. S. Lewis was talking about when he asked, "Is there any pleasure on earth as great as the circle of Christian friends by a good fire?"

Some of the pastors I interviewed emphasized how discussing problems with friends was essential for managing stress. Face-to-face interaction is ideal, of course. But with technology like Zoom and Facetime, it's now possible to keep up with good friends who live far away. Said one pastor, "One of my dearest friends was a missionary doctor in Malawi, Africa. Our regular Skype calls played a huge role in getting us both through stressful times."

One pastor specifically noted the power of his friendships:

"I think relationships are what's kept me from losing it. My wife and I have our best friends in the world in this church. I've baptized their children, watched those kids grow up, married them, and then baptized *their children*! I've buried these friend's parents. So we really are doing life together, and I think being in a place where you're doing life together, it's a stress reliever."

2. Peers/colleagues

For another pastor, meeting with men he respected, guys he could talk to and pray with was essential to keeping a healthy perspective. This isn't news. We all realize that positive collegial relationships can be a huge source of social support . . . and help us develop resilience. Pastors often experience powerful feelings of isolation and loneliness due to the unique demands of ministerial work. That's why strong peer relationships are paramount.[21]

If you don't have a senior staff member or a board member with whom you can open up, I hope you have a local pastor or two you can do that with. If not, cultivate such relationships. You'll likely experience some awkwardness and resistance at first. Why?

Because pastors are busy. And they can be competitive and/or wary. *Why is this guy wanting to go to lunch? What's his agenda?* Push through that reluctance. Hey, you might be at different churches (even in different denominations), but you're not enemies—you're on the same team. Besides, it may be that no one but another pastor will really be able to relate to the struggles you're facing.

One refreshingly candid pastor found this to be true:

"I have two close preacher friends that I can tell anything to. We will call each other up and say, 'Let me tell you what this 'rear end' did to me today. Let me tell you what he said. Let me tell you what I said.' We will just say everything we need to say and then it's done. We also go on a retreat once a year for a whole week. We have done it for twelve years now and it is something I really look forward to, because the first few days we do what you would think pastors do, planning for the next year and talk about what we're preaching through. But, after that and for the next couple of days, we just laugh and hoot and holler. We do things that are a lot of fun. Pastors can be pretty weird. Often times we're hard on each other and very competitive. I think pastors have a hard time opening up with other pastors because you just don't know if you can trust them, but these guys I can trust."

3. Confidants

Several U. S. Presidents—Andrew Jackson, Harry Truman, Ronald Reagan—created little groups (made up of trusted friends, associates, and allies) to advise them informally on various matters. Teddy Roosevelt's group was called his "tennis cabinet" because the men played tennis together to unwind.

It's smart to have a handful of people like this to whom you can vent safely and with whom you can process wisely. A sounding board is a great resource (especially if you're the kind of personality who processes out loud). Great confidants are full of grace. And they're safe. They know you don't mean certain things. They get that you're just trying to think and feel your way through difficulties.

As Dinah Craik put it:

"Oh, the comfort, the inexpressible comfort of feeling safe with a person; having neither to weigh thoughts nor measure words, but to pour them all out, just as they are, chaff and grain together, knowing that a faithful hand will take and sift them, keep what is worth keeping, and then, with a breath of kindness, blow the rest away."

NOTE: Obviously the roles of friend, colleague, and confidant can overlap.

4. Mentors/mentees

Younger pastors are now burning out and leaving the ministry in record numbers. This highlights the idea that younger pastors could benefit from the wisdom and guidance of ministers who have "been around the block a few times." As one older clergyman put it, they need to learn the rhythms:

> "Pastoral ministry is exceedingly stressful and, after being in one place for thirty-seven years, I've learned that there are certain rhythms in the life of the church, in the life of the community, and also in my own life. It is imperative to plan for those rhythms. Younger guys need to know that."

This is why experts so strongly recommend mentoring for reducing ministers' stress. Having a mentor can be a tremendous help when you are young. And, frankly, being a mentor to less experienced pastors when you are older can be a blessing too. Consider how these themes coalesce in this older pastor's comments:

> "One of my mentors used to remind me, 'If Jesus dying for the church is not enough, [then] me dying for her isn't going to help at all.' He helped me see I need to be in it for the long haul. Ministry is stressful. That's why I tell young preachers: Watch for it not only in your life but also in the life of your spouse. The two of you are a team. And if you lose her, there aren't many churches that will let you do this wonderful thing I can't believe we get paid to do."

Older pastors have developed more effective coping skills over time. Most are still pastors because of their hardiness and resiliency. What is clear is that younger pastors need mentors.[22]

Sometimes good mentors might come from your congregation. An older, wiser, Christ-like financial planner may not have any experience preaching sermons, but he can serve as a great source of wisdom when you're facing financial stressors. An older couple that has raised their children well can be invaluable as you deal with the stressors of parenting.

You never know where mentors might come from.

5. Counselors

One study found that pastors who are aware of their burnout are more likely to be involved in regular counseling. However, "more likely" doesn't mean that most weary pastors actually avail themselves of this kind of relational resource.

Consider the example of the Rural Pastors Initiative (RPI). This was a nationwide program developed and implemented by the Center for New Community (CNC) in Chicago, IL.

Designed to help rural pastors overcome some of the major challenges they face in their ministries (including loneliness and isolation, burnout, work-life imbalance, and a lack of self-care activities), the program promoted spiritual activities, social support, talk therapy, and self-care activities as strategies for dealing with stress and drawing close to God.

In terms of preventing burnout, the program was ineffective. The pastors were aware of the available resources, but most opted *not* to utilize the program. They tended to prefer activities like prayer and Bible study over talk therapy.[23]

Perhaps this is due to the unfortunate stigma many in the church place on counseling. Many consider Christians—especially Christian leaders—who engage in therapy to be spiritually suspect and/or weak. Nothing could be further from the truth. Undergoing counseling—with a trained, wise, godly therapist—when you're on the fast path to burnout is actually a sign of spiritual wisdom and strength.

Those five relationships are critical in a stress-filled world. You don't need them all…every day, but you do need people in your life you can trust and talk to, people who will laugh and cry with you, folks who will stick by you and shoot you straight.

Any plan for dealing with stress and avoiding burnout that doesn't include that is no plan at all.

QUESTIONS FOR REFLECTION / DISCUSSION

- How have you experienced loneliness in ministry?

- Do you have a group like the one Brother Charles gathers with sporadically?

- How could you take his "Festival of Meat" idea and run with it?

- This chapter mentioned various kinds of important relationships: friends, colleagues/peers, confidants, mentors, and counselors. In which categories are you strongest and weakest? Why?

- Who are your closest friends? Are they inside or outside the church?

- Do you have a peer or colleague with whom you can "let down your hair"?

- If you are a younger pastor, do you have an older pastor to turn to for advice?

- What about a mentor in some other stressful area of life?

- If you are an older pastor, are you mentoring any younger pastors?

- Are you in counseling or do you have a therapist? Why or why not?

CHAPTER 13

The Importance of Remembering

Two pastors were lamenting being in the doghouse at home:

Pastor 1: You can't believe how critical my wife is!

Pastor 1: You think *yours* is bad? Get this: Yesterday, we decided to go to the park. I remembered the stroller, the portable playpen, AND the diaper bag. But when we got there, all she could talk about was how I forgot the baby!

Forgetting important things will get you in trouble. Every single time.

Let's take a moment, then, to remember where we've been so far. In the first half of this book, we looked at the growing problem of pastoral stress and burnout.

Here in the second half of this book, we're talking about some practical steps you can take when ministry gets stressful and you feel like you are riding a cruise missile straight to trouble.

In chapter 10, we looked at *preventable* stressors—things in your life you can eliminate in short order. In chapter 11, we discussed the restorative power of walking away from work and taking time off—really OFF—to unwind and recharge. In the last chapter, we noted the huge role that close relationships can play in helping us navigate life's crazy times.

In this chapter, we want to look at the powerful habit of *remembering*. Because we are so prone to forget, we must engage in the practice of remembering.

When I tell you that I am a forgetful person, it is an understatement. I once got in my car to go to work and realized that I forgot something inside. So, I got out of my car and walked through my house into my bedroom and into my closet. As I stepped into the closet and began to look around, I thought to myself, *What was it I came in here for?*

That's right. I forgot what I forgot. And let me just say that when you get to the point that you can say, "I forgot what I forgot," you can be qualified as a forgetful person.

Can you relate at all?

There is a Greek word we all are familiar with. It's *amnesia*. It means "forgetfulness."

Forgetfulness is not simply a problem in the physical realm. It's also common (and even more dangerous) in the spiritual realm. Worse than forgetting something for work or a friend's birthday is when we forgot what God has told us, taught us, or done for us, and it begins to affect us in our current circumstances. We get overwhelmed or anxious, or even worse, we feel compelled to do something to try to save ourselves or change an outcome.

One author said:

"...the Christian life is a combination of amnesia and déja vu."

"I know I've forgotten this before."

Can you relate?! Of course, you can. This is a common experience for everyone who has ever followed Christ.

We forget God's goodness, graciousness, faithfulness, provision, etc... etc... only to obsess over a new set of stressors in our life that are sure to baffle him and ruin us.

Or even worse, in the times of goodness and plenty and peace, we forget that every good gift is from above.

Ever been there?!?

Yes, we sometimes suffer from spiritual amnesia. This becomes evident when we have to learn the same lessons over and over again.

But there is an alternative to amnesia… it is what the Greeks called *anamnesis*.

While we sometimes suffer from spiritual amnesia, we can benefit from spiritual anamnesis.

Anamnesis is the act of "bringing certain realities to one's memory." It's more than just recalling factual information. It's remembering the past in such a way that it empowers the present. This kind of remembering is more than nostalgia, it's life-changing!

Our enemy would love us to live 24/7 with spiritual amnesia. Because when we relive how God, in his grace and love has freed us and moved in our lives, we are dangerous to him.

So, remembering is hugely important. No wonder Moses, in his final words to the nation of Israel (i.e., the Book of Deuteronomy), urged again and again, "Remember . . . . remember . . . remember." And just in case anyone in the crowd was dozing off, he also expressed it this way, "Don't forget . . . don't forget . . . don't forget."

Let's look at three categories of things pressure-packed preachers need to bring to their minds regularly to stave off discouragement:

1. Remembering what's true

2. Remembering your calling

3. Remembering God's faithfulness

1. Remembering What's True

Here are some truths—some hard to swallow, some encouraging—every pastor needs to embrace.

- Stress is inevitable. (We live in a fallen world.)

- Contrary to popular belief, God *will* often give us more than *we* can handle. (That's so we will turn to Him and cast our cares on Him.) However, He will never give us more than we can handle *when we are relying on Him.*

- Though stress will never completely disappear this side of heaven, some stressors are only for a season. (Remember your grandma saying, "This too will pass"?)

- Self-care is *not* selfishness. (If you go down, you'll be of no use to anyone else.)

- To survive, the church you serve does not *need* you to be available 24/7. (You're not the Messiah. You can go to sleep, trusting that God is awake.)

- Perfectionism is an unhealthy—and futile—goal. (There is no greater frustration than being an imperfect perfectionist.)

- "Success" in ministry + failure at home = failure (Save yourself future regret by making your family top priority.)

- It's far better to wear out gradually, than to flame out in a scandalous way. (Pace yourself, and by God's grace, you won't end up being a cautionary tale for other believers.)

- You have all the time you need to do all the things God has called you to do. (Where God guides, he provides.)

- With practice, you can transform some of your stress into motivation. (Remember *eustress?*)

- With a healthy *perspective* and by *modifying* your behavior and *adopting* self-care practices, you can go the distance!

It's actually a wise idea to keep a list like this handy and to re-read it daily. By constantly reviewing these truths and preaching these affirmations to your own heart, you'll avoid some heartache.

2. Remembering Your Calling

When you're stuck in the middle of a difficult season, stress is especially scary. But we don't have to let it have the last word. Let me include some encouragement here before we go on.

There's a reason you're in ministry today.

Think back to the first time you sensed a divine prompting to ministry. Think of all the discernment it took you to get to this point. The place to which your calling has led you might be stressful, but the fact that once upon a time you sensed an unmistakable divine call can be a solace and an anchor in times of doubt.

Like other ministers, you went into ministry to use your gifts (both spiritual and natural) in helping to build Christ's church. Leading people to Jesus. Leading Christians to more compassionate and holy lives. At least one pastor I interviewed found this notion of calling to be essential to his longevity in ministry:

> "I didn't want to be a pastor; I wanted to be a lawyer. I tell people all the time: 'I didn't want to save people; I wanted to sue them!' But God had different ideas. So many times in my ministry I wanted to throw in the towel and leave. The only thing that kept me in the game was the fact that I was convinced God had called me to that place."

Thus, a pastor's calling can be a source of motivation in the toughest times. Unless and/or until God clearly calls you to do something else, you have the assurance you are in the right place.

Again, there are different kinds of stress and different sources of stress. Sometimes stress comes from those who are antagonistic to your ministry. Sometimes it comes from counseling situations, where you know that you could help someone, but they won't do what you asked them to do. Those are completely different kinds of stress, and you have to handle them differently. I don't know which one is easier to handle. I just know that remembering your calling can ground you.

One of the pastors I spoke with told me with great passion:

"It's God's call that's going to keep you there. I can go back and show you the spot in the choir in my home church where, on a Saturday night, I surrendered to preach. It's as vivid as if it happened yesterday, and it's been sixty-seven years now. If I didn't have that sure knowledge that God called me, I wouldn't have made it."

By recalling your calling, you can even be satisfied even amid stress. However, don't take my word for it. Consider the findings of a large study of almost 750 Presbyterian pastors. The survey found the majority of the clergy had some degree of burnout. Forty percent reported a mild case. Twenty-five percent reported moderate burnout, and seven percent reported a high degree of burnout.

More than a third showed signs of emotional exhaustion, lost enthusiasm, feelings of being drained by their various ministry roles. And yet despite routine feelings of fatigue and frustration, the overwhelming majority of the pastors surveyed said they felt a strong sense of accomplishment and high levels of satisfaction in ministry!

Ninety-one percent of these Presbyterian pastors said they were satisfied because they positively impacted people's lives. *Eighty-four percent said they were glad they answered God's call and entered the ministry.*

Notice, these pastors reported feelings of satisfaction *and* burnout. At the same time! In other words, high satisfaction *can* coexist with heavy stress. And those high levels of satisfaction aren't sure-fire protection against wearing out or flaming out. In short, the study highlights a pastor's need for a strategic plan that can reduce the negative effects of stress and enhance ministry satisfaction.[24]

If you haven't experienced this yet, you will: Chronic Stress is an equal opportunity enemy. It hits when you're struggling—and when you're successful. Ironically, times of great victory can sometimes be even more stressful than when everything is going wrong. (For a biblical example of this, remember the curious case of Elijah the prophet in 1 Kings 18-19.)

Before moving to our third item for remembering, let me say a word about the importance of longevity. When the stress is severe, and the desire to quit is strong, it's wise to remember the value of sticking it out. Hanging around. Outlasting the critics.

Consider the results of another interesting study, this time of 285 evangelical pastors. Thirty-six percent of the respondents were between the ages of 35 and 49. (These, the study concluded, tend to be the most challenging years for pastors.) Thirty-four percent of these pastors were serving in their first church, while a majority (fifty-three percent) were serving their second or third congregations.

Drilling deeper, we find these interesting tidbits: Fifty-five percent of these evangelical pastors reported their churches' attendance had recently declined or plateaued. And twenty-eight percent were leading a church that had forced a pastor to resign at some point.

Serving a church that has experienced trauma like that is almost guaranteed to generate more stress for a pastor. Often affected church members have "buried" the intense emotions surrounding such ordeals (i.e., staff changes, splits, power struggles, scandals, etc.). When a new pastor comes along and innocently, unknowingly triggers old, unresolved memories, the result is rarely pretty. What am I saying here? Congregational trauma is a real thing.

And burnout is particularly high among pastors who serve "traumatized" churches. So is the desire to leave for greener pastures. But consider this pastor's wise perspective:

"You're always going to have negative people in your church, but oftentimes they're not against you personally. You know why the average church pastor has people that are always cantankerous and suspicious? It's because on average they lose a pastor every three years. And they have to live with that, and with whatever else that pastor did, good or bad."

You've seen it. Maybe you've experienced it. The old guy moves on. The new guy comes in and tries to do something significant and the people *revolt*! It's not because the new pastor is a bad guy, or because the congregation is mean or they dislike him personally. Often it's because they're wounded. Or they're fearful he'll change their church even more than the last guy, then bolt for a bigger church. (Barna Research reports that the average pastor serves mainline congregations for only about four years.[25])

No wonder it sometimes takes a while for a flock to warm up to a new pastor. They're the ones that will have to deal with the mess and fallout when he's gone.

Thus the power of not only remembering your calling but remembering the power of longevity. Sticking around. Settling in. Putting down roots. That's how you build trust with your people. You can't do it in a few months. It only happens over the long haul.

Longevity brings incredible benefits to ministry. Some of the older, veteran pastors I interviewed wondered if some pastors burnout because they leave stressful churches too quickly when exciting new opportunities came along. One said:

> "Periodically, there are times when you can either get a new call to a new church or you can renew your call to the church that you're already in. I'm afraid many pastors come to a tough spot and they opt to bail out and go somewhere else. They forget that every church has its challenges, every church has negative people, every church has things that make it an imperfect church."

Another added: "Many pastors get weary and then move from church to church. I am not saying that every move is premature, but I'm persuaded that quite a few of them are. They're thinking, 'Well, if I can just go to another church, I know it will be better there.' It won't be. The enemy is at work there, too. He's going to follow you wherever you go."

Two things are true about the decision to go or stay: One, by moving you might be swapping one set of problems for an even bigger set. Two, things can change if you stick around. As one pastor told me, "When it comes to dealing with people, I decided early on that when I had to deal with difficult people, I was either going to 'outlove' them or 'outlast' them. I wasn't going to let them push my buttons. I wasn't going to let them make me angry."

I've learned this lesson: The things that make you angry in your first year of ministry may not faze you ten years in.

The final thing to remember—when stress is big and burnout seems imminent…

3. Remembering God's Faithfulness

When times are bleak, nothing can buoy your spirit more than a mental review of all the times and all the ways God has shown up big in your life.

This is where a journal can be so precious. When you jot down answered prayers…keep a list of changed lives…describe unexpected blessings…document incidents of undeserved favor, you have an awe-inspiring record of divine faithfulness.

Look back at all the baptisms. The life-changing conversations. The healed marriages. The sovereign circumstances that produced wonderful fruit. If God did all this in the past, and if he's a God who never changes, why wouldn't he continue to do such things in the future?

I am not a very sentimental person, but maybe I am a selective hoarder because I have every handwritten note anyone has ever given me. I have saved every letter, every picture, every expression of love or appreciation that my kids or my wife have ever given me.

For my 15th anniversary, the church was offered the opportunity to write me notes of appreciation for those 15 years. I cherish those. Some were from new people, and some came from families that had been with the church from the very beginning.

I still have those cards. I keep them in a basket in my office. Every so often, when I start to feel discouraged or tired or "forgetful," I take a few of the cards and read them. They're proof that God is always at work, often in ways we can't see at the time.

The notes remind me that God has called me to these people, at this time, to serve them and see them grow in Christ. He has been faithful, and He will continue to be faithful. Remembering like this is unbelievably powerful and rejuvenating!

Many of the psalms are like these cards. They are simple remembrances of God's jaw-dropping faithfulness. No wonder God's ancient people loved to sing them so often!

Let me close with a powerful memory from my own ministry.

When we started the process of planting the church I'm at now, I had a sinking feeling of "What the heck have I gotten myself into?"

I had been a youth minister at my home church—the church in which I grew up, was baptized and called to ministry. I was more than comfortable. I had a steady paycheck—more than I ever thought I could make being a youth minister. I had a 401(k), health insurance, and a staff that consisted of a full-time administrative assistant, a full-time ministry assistant, plus a brood of interns.

When I followed the call to plant a church, I left all of that behind. No staff, no paycheck, no insurance, no office, no building. Plus I emptied my 401(k) to have enough money to live on until the church could get on its feet.

On top of all that, I had recently gotten married. Imagine my wife's excitement when, eight months into a fairly stable marriage, I created a wave of instability! (I'm sure she also thought, *What have I gotten myself into?*)

I had the full blessing of my pastor and my home church. Even so, there were still a lot of questions. People wondered why I was leaving, why I was starting another church. I remember coming to the realization that I would never be able to answer every question or quell every rumor. The experience was very isolating.

A month later, in January, I found myself at a church conference in Michigan. (Did you catch that? A church conference in *January* . . . in *Michigan*! Who *plans* such a thing? Who *attends* such an event?)

My hotel was directly across the parking lot from the church hosting the conference. As I walked through the fresh snow—about 8 inches deep—I began to think about how alone I felt.

Depression began to set in. As I got to the door of the church I looked back from where I had come, and I saw the distinctive track of boot prints I had left behind. It was like a huge, calm sea of snow disturbed only by my walking through it. It was then that it hit me, *I am all alone... what am I doing? I can't do this. I don't know how to do this!*

And that's when I felt God speak to me softly, "You are *not* alone, I am with you... I will *not* leave you alone."

During the next few days of the conference, I kept writing in my journal, "How am I going to do this?" I think I must have written that question at least 10 different times over three days.

On the final day, God answered that question. I immediately wrote what I sensed him saying in my conference notebook.

Here's what I jotted down, "You are not going to do this, I am. Stay out of My way." That was so freeing for me, it became my motto. "Stay out of God's way." I live by that thought even today.

Fast forward about five years. I went back to the same conference, at the same church, during the same month (Yes, for some reason they kept having their conference in Michigan in January!).

But, in those years, the church had grown, because God kept doing amazing things. With me on this trip were four staff members who had since joined our team. I remember as we rode to the hotel (the same one I had stayed at previously), snow was falling. In fact, it snowed all night.

We got up the next morning and walked across that same snow-covered parking lot. As we got to the door to walk in, I looked back at the path we took from our hotel to the church. Where five years prior there had only been one set of prints, now there were five. I was overcome as I remembered what God had spoken to me in that dark, lonely time of uncertainty five years prior… "I will not leave you alone."

Remembering God's faithfulness can make all the difference.

QUESTIONS FOR REFLECTION / DISCUSSION

- On a typical day, how forgetful are you? What's the biggest thing you've ever forgotten? (Hopefully not your baby.)

- Do you agree that the active, intentional habit of remembering certain truths can help when life is stressful? Why or why not?

- What other "truths about stress and burnout" would you add to the list in this chapter?

- Talk about your "calling" into full-time vocational ministry. How might that be an anchor in stressful times?

- What are the pros and cons of staying in one church for the long haul?

- When have you been most blown away by God's faithfulness to you?

CHAPTER 14

Stewarding Your One and Only Body

In one of the (many!) great scenes from the classic movie *The Princess Bride*, the evil Prince Humperdinck is clearly stressed. He begins to recite all the things on his to-do list: "I've got my country's 500th anniversary to plan, my wedding to arrange, my wife to murder, and Guilder to blame for it. I'm swamped."

His henchman, the six-fingered Count Rugen, looks at him and says softly, "Get some rest. If you haven't got your health, you haven't got anything."

It's a silly scene in an even sillier movie. Yet Count Rugen's statement is right on the money. Without your health, you're sunk! You can't have much of a life, and you sure can't have a vibrant ministry.

THE PHYSICAL HEALTH OF PASTORS

As I mentioned back in chapter two, in my conversations with pastors, about 40 percent mentioned having some sort of physical ailment due to stress.

Several reported *digestive problems*. One said,

"Most of my life, I've been very healthy. Rarely sick with a 'go-to-the doctor' kind of illness. I never had ulcers or any of that stuff. But the last couple of years, I've had a bad case of acid reflux. I'm pretty sure it's church-induced and stress-related. Maybe it's partly due to all the coffee I drink, but I think it's mostly the result of stress."

Another echoed that diagnosis:

"From a young age, I was a Type A personality, driven, and perfectionistic. And I internalized all that intensity. I sent it to my colon and got ulcerative colitis when I was fourteen! It just about killed me. The doctors figured out what it was, and got it under control until I was twenty-eight and in ministry. Once again I found myself dealing with major health issues. I was probably forty or forty-two before we got it under control again. For me, stress usually goes right there to my gut."

Some, because of pastoral pressures, said they battle *insomnia*. One pastor told me: "I still struggle at times with insomnia. When it's bad, I typically only sleep about four to five hours a night. This morning I woke up at 3:30, thinking *Man, we got to do this and this and this and this and this...*"

Does this describe you? Do you have trouble *falling* asleep...or *staying* asleep?

Some complained of *high blood pressure*. One described how a rocky start at his church did a serious number on his health:

"Because I was getting strong opposition from two powerful leaders on staff, I developed high blood pressure. I was sweating through my suits, and I couldn't sleep at night. I even started losing my hair! The stress was just unrelenting. Finally, after I'd been there about six months those two staff members up and resigned. (Of course, they had to blast me on their way out.)"

Sexual dysfunction was cited as another unwanted physical consequence of excessive stress. One minister bravely admitted," I know a lot of pastors don't like to talk about this, but if you bring stress with you into the bedroom it will affect you there."

Others mentioned *weight gain* due to stress-related eating. They spoke of trying to find pleasure in food or eating for comfort. Said one: "I've always struggled with weight. I can tell I'm under a great deal of pressure. I catch myself thinking, *Man, I just want to go eat!* When I get like that, my wrong idea of a balanced meal is a Big Mac in each hand! If I let myself, I could just eat and eat. That is one of the unhealthy ways that I have dealt with stress."

Another added: "I struggled with my weight my whole time in ministry. I'm fifty pounds less now than I was when I retired. What happens when you have a high-stress, high-demand job? Most guys respond by being workaholics. Some turn to food."

When the pressure is extreme and there's no plan to address it other than to double down and push harder, even more serious health problems can arise. One pastor said with a deep sigh:

> "I had something called a spontaneous cerebral fluid leak. (I think 'spontaneous' is the word doctors use when don't have any idea why something happened). I'm convinced it was stress-related.

> "Stress is funny. The effects often don't hit you until later. You go through a stressful period, get past it, and think, *Whew, we made it through! That's good.* Then about three weeks later, you're in trouble!"

Another mentioned his own serious health scare: "Early on in ministry, I was burning the candle at both ends. I didn't want to stop. I just wanted to know where I could get more wax! I ended up with *pneumonia*. Now, as I look back, I think it was kind of a chastisement from God."

Perhaps he's right. In the 23rd Psalm, David referenced how the Lord "*makes* me lie down in green pastures" (emphasis added). Maybe when we get too important in our own minds, too big for our ministry britches, God, in love, says, "Since you won't do it yourself, I will *make* you stop and get some rest."

Let's look briefly at some practical ways we can deal with stress and guard our physical health.

STRESS RELIEF THROUGH EATING RIGHT

Relax. This *isn't* a book about calories, carbs, or crunches. The last thing you need is a lecture from me about the dangers of obesity.

Besides, with hundreds of diet fads and eating plans out there (and new ones coming out all the time), there might be more opinions about eating than there are people in the world!

Nevertheless, here are some things I bet we can all agree on:

- We only get one body in this life. Therefore, it makes sense to take good care of it.

- Regular medical check-ups are smart.

- Food is a fantastic gift from God.

- As with any good gift (e.g., sex, money, hobbies, etc.), we can view and use food inappropriately.

- From a divine perspective, food seems designed to supply us with nutrition and energy and pleasure. (Otherwise, why did God give us taste buds, and why does the Bible constantly advocate meals and feasts with family and friends?).

- Unhealthy food issues emerge when we look to food to provide us with things it was never intended to provide. In short, we should eat when we're physically hungry…not when we're sad, nervous, bored, or in need of comfort. One pastor admitted, "I have a bad habit of wolfing down my food—and because of that,

I often overeat. Before my food 'lands' in my stomach and can signal my brain, 'That's enough!' I've usually overdone it! I eat too fast and I eat too much."

- Gaining and carrying too much weight puts stress on your joints and your organs.

- When you're at your ideal weight, you just feel better physically. (Emotionally too—i.e., you have more confidence.)

- When we consume more calories than we burn over a period of time, we soon find ourselves in the market for a bigger belt.

In reference to eating, one pastor said:

"As I've gotten older, I've totally changed—not my diet so much, as my lifestyle. Diets don't work—you've got to make a lifestyle change. So there are certain things I just don't eat anymore: bread, sweets, fried foods, I just kind of watch what I eat. As a result, I've dropped twenty-five pounds in the last year. My goal isn't losing weight so much as keeping it off."

STRESS RELIEF THROUGH EXERCISE

Here was an interesting finding: Of the older, wiser pastors I spoke with, the majority said they relieved stress through exercise.

One of them said that during his most hectic seasons of ministry, "I never sacrificed exercising five or six days a week for an hour. I jogged. I ran. And I worked out with weights." He went on to mention that unless he was exercising with someone else, he used that workout time to consciously be with the Lord in prayer and meditation.

Another pastor told me, "In the years I was running, which was about thirty years, I ran 1,500 miles a year minimum. Not only did I stay in good shape, but I also had energy. I truly believe that energy expended makes energy that comes back into you again. Give and it comes back to you."

The good thing about exercise is that there are countless ways to get your body moving. If you don't like certain activities, that's fine. You don't have to do those things. Find something you *do* enjoy, and do it habitually. A former pastor, now in his sixties, says, "I can't do so many of the things I used to do. Weights. Running. Racquetball. Basketball. I miss those things, but I also know I can't just sit around and watch my belly expand. So I walk 5-6 miles a day. I pray, think, and listen to podcasts. It's become one of my favorite outlets."

STRESS RELIEF THROUGH SLEEP

The pastors I spoke with also emphasized sleep as a great remedy for stress. Said one: "You know the first thing that God did when Elijah was running from Jezebel? He provided some food and told him to eat and get some sleep. You know, a little rest and a little nourishment."

Another cited the same biblical story concerning the need for sleep, saying:

A long time ago I was studying the story of Elijah in 1 Kings 19. You know it. One day the prophet's calling down fire from heaven. The next day he's running from Jezebel, praying to die! What I learned from that story is that God took care of his physical needs before he addressed Elijah's emotional and spiritual needs....When I get necessary rest, it's amazing how much more effective I am."

It's worth noting that the field of sleep science has made huge strides in recent years. We understand more than ever about the mystery of sleep. And we're learning what things facilitate or hinder a good night's rest. My point is: If you're struggling in this area, real help is available.

One pastor noted that his stress plan included good sleep combined with exercise: "I've worked out religiously ever since I was young, almost every day. And I try to get plenty of sleep. If I get about six and a half hours of sleep, maybe seven, I'm good. I can't sleep more than that."

From my vantage point, younger pastors are often more aware of the importance of maintaining their physical health. Generally speaking, it seems to me they are more likely to incorporate healthy eating and regular exercise into their daily lives. I do know that the ones who *don't* develop these habits early on will pay when they grow older.

I sense that older pastors tend to struggle more in these areas. So let me say something to the good shepherds like Pastor Ken who sacrifice so much for their flocks.

Remember Ken? He gets up early and goes to bed late. He spends hours and hours at his desk reading and praying and preparing sermons. As we've mentioned, Ken's diet isn't great. He's always on the run, grabbing a meal here, going through a fast-food drive-through there. He eats a lot of breakfasts and lunches with parishioners. And Ken doesn't really exercise regularly. No wonder all his suits are tight.

Pastor, if you're like Ken, I want you to think about what you're sacrificing by working so hard. Maybe it seems selfish to take an hour to go to the gym...especially when there are so many other things you need to get done.

I remind you that as pastors we're called to sacrifice our egos, not our wellbeing. Maybe one day you *will* be asked to sacrifice your body for the sake of the gospel. However, I don't believe God will ever ask you to forsake your health just so your staff or board or congregation will think you're a hard worker.

That's not martyrdom, that's messed-up thinking.

Being physically healthy matters. When the ministry gets crazy (and it always does) a good diet, regular exercise, and restful sleep can be a lifeline.

Count Rugen, with his six-fingers, was right: "If you haven't got your health, you haven't got anything."

QUESTIONS FOR REFLECTION / DISCUSSION

- In what ways—if any—do you misuse (or abuse) food—especially when you're under a lot of pressure?

- Do you agree that turning to food for comfort is unhealthy? Why or why not?

- What, if anything, needs to change in your relationship to food?

- On a scale of 1-10 (with one being "I haven't exerted myself physically since George W. Bush was President" and 10 being "If you saw one of my workouts, you'd think I was an Olympic athlete") how would you rate yourself when it comes to exercise?

- What exercises have you found to de-stress, and even energize you?

- Describe your sleep habits. Do you get enough rest? Is it solid? Do you wake up refreshed?

- What's the biggest thing you're taking away from this chapter?

CHAPTER 15

Cultivating Holy Habits

How do those pro athletes do it?

Case in point, the star NBA guard who steps to the foul line with one second left on the clock. He grins, then calmly swishes two free throws to send the game into overtime.

Or take that lanky, largely unknown 27-year-old who's leading the Masters by one shot. He strides to the 18th tee at Augusta on Sunday afternoon. With all the pressure in the world on his shoulders, he uncorks a 320-yard drive straight down the middle of the fairway! Seemingly unfazed, he then sticks his approach shot 20 feet from the pin. Two putts and twenty minutes later, he's slipping on a coveted green jacket!

Or consider the All-Pro defensive end that's been invisible all game. Late in the fourth quarter, he uses a bull rush, then a textbook swim move to get past his blocker. The result is a clutch "strip sack" that gives his team the ball and a chance to win in the game's waning moments.

Where do these guys get the resolve, the confidence, and the ability to meet such pressure-packed moments so successfully?

They get those qualities and skills from hours and hours of practice. They've trained their bodies and minds to respond to whatever the game throws at them.

THE POWER OF SPIRITUAL DISCIPLINES

This is why it's so important for us as pastors to train our *souls*. The Apostle Paul told his young protégé, Timothy, this very thing when he urged, "Train yourself to be godly" (1 Timothy 4:7, NIV). The verb Paul employed in that verse is the Greek word from which we get our English word *gymnasium*. Clearly, the apostle wanted his young pastor friend to picture athletes working out, building endurance and strength, getting ready for a challenging competition.

In so many words, Paul was saying, "Timothy, in the same way that a great athlete prepares his body, you can get your heart and mind in tip-top shape. Except, instead of physical exercises, you'll need to engage in spiritual ones."

Whether we call these training exercises for the heart/mind/soul "spiritual disciplines," "spiritual practices," or "engaging in spiritual formation," the goal is to be consistent. That's the only way to be prepared. Great athletes don't just train once in a blue moon, or whenever they *feel* like it. They're in the gym every day. In the same way, pastors who want to be able to withstand stress have to do spiritual exercises regularly.

It's vital to remember that we don't train spiritually to "impress God" (and certainly not other people). We do spiritual exercises to draw near to God. Why? Because it's there, in his life-changing presence that we find all we need to face whatever life is throwing at us.

What kind of spiritual activities are we talking about? Familiar ones like prayer, Bible reading, fasting, Scripture memory, biblical meditation, enjoying Sabbath rest, solitude, and silence. (That's far from an exhaustive list. Many spiritual leaders engage in other soul-shaping activities like accountability, retreats, devotional reading, journaling, spiritual direction, and simplicity.)

We see many of these spiritual activities in the pages of Scripture. We see others in the lives of devout believers down through church history.

What we can say for sure is these disciplines are tried and true. They do indeed lead us to the peace and love of the Savior.

To recap, here's what we're saying: In the same way that intense training helps athletes gain mental toughness, physical strength, and "muscle memory" so they don't wilt under pressure when facing big moments, rigorous spiritual training can equip pastors for the stressors of ministry and life.

If the Bible *commands* spiritual disciplines, then research *commends* them. One study of 270 pastors found that forty-one percent had experienced burnout out due to emotional exhaustion. The researchers also discovered a strong connection between emotional exhaustion and the condition of spiritual dryness (defined as "depletion of spiritual vitality"). They concluded that "ongoing spiritual renewal" is the best safeguard against this.[26]

In other words, engaging in spiritual disciplines (i.e., "ongoing spiritual renewal") gives religious workers an advantage against stress and burnout—and may be the only way out of spiritual dryness. When we participate in spiritual exercises, we obviously cannot *force* God to act. However, we can put ourselves (and our souls) in situations to receive His grace.

Having a commitment to read the Bible and pray daily can help ministers deal with stress. One pastor said:

> "In seminary, because I was reading and discussing the Bible and theology all day, every day, I quit having a 'quiet time.' It wasn't long before my spiritual life was all head and no heart."

> "Then early in my ministry, I did it again. I started skipping my devotional time. I rationalized that I was praying for people all the time, and I was spending many hours each week in sermon prep. Sure enough, it wasn't long before I noticed I was feeling distant from God—and getting impatient with people. Eventually, it clicked: My prayers and Bible study had become

part of 'my job description.' I was doing lots *for* God, but I wasn't consciously being *with* him. I was neglecting my own heart. And it showed."

"So I remember I started spending time in the Psalms every morning. Just reading them thoughtfully and reflecting on them. And praying them for myself. The difference was amazing!"

Another pastor I spoke with talked about how having daily devotions reduced stress in his marriage:

"One of the things my wife and I committed to doing is to read the Scripture together and pray every day. The more we do that, the less I get in trouble. I have not been on the sofa in twelve months. I've been in my bed! I have often been known to be on the sofa."

We've talked in previous pages about the importance of rest, specifically the need to take a "Sabbath" day off. This practice—if you do it routinely—is a powerful safeguard against burnout.

Again, observing a Sabbath doesn't mean you have to cease working from Friday sundown to Saturday sundown. (I can hear some preachers saying, "How could I possibly do that when I have to preach several times each weekend?")

Each minister has to find his own time to unplug and disengage. I only know that if you are preoccupied with work 24/7, you are at risk of emotional exhaustion and burnout. No one can be on the clock around the clock. That is the way of Pharaoh.

No, we refrain from working on one day of the week to remind ourselves of our dependence on God. On that day we rest, relax, recharge, rejoice. But, it needs to be contextual. Each pastor and/or church will have a different schedule.

Here's how one pastor worked it out:

"I tell my staff, 'If you work six days, you get two days off.' And they think I'm bad at math. But here's what I mean: I go in at 6:30 in the morning when most everyone else goes in at 8:30 in the morning. So, I beat them by two hours on Monday, Tuesday, Wednesday, and Thursday. And some of those days, I also have things in the evening. My point is this: if you get in the habit of going in early you can gain eight hours of work, a whole day. Because I go in early and stay late some days, I can take Friday and Saturday off and not feel the least bit guilty about it because, hours-wise, I am working the equivalent of six days."

AND IF A PASTOR REFUSES TO PRACTICE THE DISCIPLINE OF REST?

When I asked the pastors I interviewed about their most stressful experiences in ministry, they often told me about times when they were *not* engaging in this regular, holy practice of rest. One pastor described the energy he needed for ministry and how stressed he became when he ran out of it:

"I've always defined stress as the gap between the demands of ministry and the strength you have to meet those demands. The Bible says in John 5, that John the Baptist was a shining and burning light. You really can't shine without burning; it's impossible. If a person is effective, then there's something going out of him. When I preach, something's going out of me. When I am ministering, something's going out of me. When people need help, something's going out of me."

You don't have to be a genius to realize that if you are constantly pouring yourself out, then you'd better be intentional about getting refilled!

As one old West Texas preacher put it, "You need to sit near the spout where the glory runs out."

Here is how another pastor explained a difficult season he endured years ago:

> "Our church was growing rapidly and we had to continue add-
> ing services. Back then there wasn't anything like video over-
> flow or satellite campuses. We didn't have that yet. What we
> did seemed to be the easiest solution. It was Saturday night,
> three times Sunday morning, Sunday night, and then Monday
> morning at seven o'clock. I did that for seven years. On top of
> that, we had countless building committee meetings to plan a
> 450,000 square-foot, 146 acre, $82 million campus. Now *that*
> is stress!"

Again, this is what spiritual practices are for. They're not a "have to." They're a "get to"! It's in doing them that we draw near to the One who has all power and peace. And when you are relying on his infinite supply, you are better equipped to face the pressures of leading a flock.

The irony is that when we're busy, it's easy to tell ourselves, "I don't have time for that." Don't fall for that trap! Maybe that's why Martin Luther allegedly said, "I have so much to do today that I shall spend the first three hours in prayer."

All the spiritual disciplines are important, but rest is critical in deal-ing with stress. A habitual lack of rest will catch up to you. Again, as one pastor said, "That's why I tell pastors that sometimes, the most spiritual thing you can do is to take a nap. We all need to rest." In fact, one study showed that feeling rested and renewed had *the greatest impact on avoiding burnout*.[27]

Sometimes a longer rest is warranted. That's why it's always wise when a church board creates policies that make it possible for their senior pastoral staff to take a sabbatical (a purposeful, structured time off for refreshment). Everyone benefits. One pastor told me:

"In our church, we have a sabbatical policy now. You have to write it up and show us what your plan is. How is this focused time off going to benefit your rest and renewal, your professional development, your marriage, your spiritual growth? What books are you going to read? There needs to be a lot of intentionality in a sabbatical."

Other spiritual practices—like spiritual reading—can help resist stress and build a healthier perspective. One veteran pastor said, "You need to read an old book every now and then—something that wasn't written in the past twenty years. Listen to what some older saints said and how they said it."

He's got a point. When's the last time you read a spiritual classic like John Milton's *Paradise Lost*, Augustine's *Confessions*, Brother Lawrence's *The Practice of the Presence of God*, or George MacDonald's *Diary of an Old Soul*.

In summary, when we engage in spiritual practices, we are emulating our Savior. Jesus, the eternal and infinite Son of God, routinely devoted time to solitude and prayer.[28] If, during his earthly ministry, he saw the need for them, how much more do we need them? Spiritual practices such as Bible study, contemplation, and prayer promote physical, psychological, and spiritual renewal and growth. Taking scheduled vacations or sabbaticals can give pastors a chance to rest, relax, and reflect.

Unfortunately, you will never *find* time for these things. And no one is going to insert these practices into your schedule for you. If you feel such activities are important to your spiritual sanity and survival, you are going to have to *make* time for them.

The only question is: "Will you do it?"

When I started out in ministry my mom told me something I've never forgotten. It was sound, godly advice. She said, "It's not special people in special places at special times that have the greatest impact for the

Kingdom of God. It is everyday people, in everyday places, who have the guts to live for Jesus every day. They are the ones who get the job done."

Not sure where she got that from, but I am so glad that she shared that with me. Don't forget, we often find the Holy in what appears to be mundane!

QUESTIONS FOR REFLECTION / DISCUSSION

- How would you explain "spiritual disciplines" to a third grader?

- What sorts of regular spiritual exercises do you engage in?

- What spiritual practices do you think would be most helpful to you right now—and what keeps you from engaging in them?

- What do you do for your devotional time? Is it hard for you to keep up this habit? Why or why not?

- Why do you think it's so hard for so many pastors to take time to rest?

- What are you reading right now—and what insights are you gaining from that reading?

CHAPTER 16
Protecting Your Wife and Kids

In the same way that bombs cause collateral damage…in the same way that a condo fire affects all the condos around it…

A pastor's stress and burnout impacts those closest to him.

In other words, if you consistently bring home all the pressures and negativity of ministry, it *will* affect the lives of your loved ones.

So what practical steps can you take to protect your wife and kids from the relentless pressures and strains of ministry? That's what we want to address briefly in this chapter.

The ministry veterans I surveyed shared eight specific things you can do:

1. Take care of yourself.
Your family is a primary reason you need to take care of yourself. Protect yourself and you protect them. Think about it: What happens to your wife and kids if you go down? If you're a burned-out wreck of your former self, where does that leave your family?

As flight attendants tell us just before takeoff, in the event of an emergency, put the oxygen mask on yourself first. That way you'll be in a position to better care for those around you. You can spare your family needless pain by taking care of yourself.

This is precisely why Solomon urged in Proverbs 4:23, "Above all else, guard your heart, for everything you do flows from it." If you carry around a lot of negativity, it will flow out of you. If you're all out of love and peace and joy, you won't be able to minister to anyone, even those who mean the most to you.

2. Look at life through your family members' eyes.

Unless you are a preacher's kid (PK)…or were previously married to a pastor and then underwent gender assignment (highly doubtful), it will be hard for you to understand how difficult it is being the wife or child of a pastor. So make the effort to see life through their eyes. Walk a mile in their shoes. Then realize this ugly truth:

Many churches are unfair to pastors' wives and children.

They often put impossible expectations on them. They hold them to ridiculously high standards.

When Chucky Churchmember's third-grader acts out, it's just a case of "kids being kids." Nobody bats an eye. But let *the pastor's* nine-year-old have a meltdown in the church courtyard between services, and watch what happens. At some churches, there will be an emergency board meeting that night! There the pastor's parenting skills and spiritual authority will be called into question.

One pastor I spoke with was refreshingly candid with his flock:

"Preachers' kids are just like anyone else's knucklehead kids. They are going to make mistakes. They're going to mess up. But just let them be kids. Every now and then I had to confront the lofty expectations people put on my kids. When they got to high school, I had to remind people, 'They are just like your kids. Don't put them on a pedestal.'"

Sigh. It may not be fair, but it's true: Pastors' families live in a fishbowl. Therefore…

3. Set boundaries with your church.

Be proactive in this. I have to be honest. This is a difficult road to navigate. But we *must* navigate it, and we must do it courageously, as this pastor did:

> "As a young pastor, I was so protective of my wife and kids that the first four churches I went to I told the search committee, 'I want you to know my wife is not the associate pastor. You do not get two for the price of one. She will be involved, but she is not going to do any more than your wives do.'

> "I also told them that my boys were going to be just like their kids. I told them, 'They're going to kiss girls and get in fights. And if they're worse than that, it will probably be because they were hanging around *your* kids.' I told them I would not let them make *weirdos* out of my family.

> "Looking back on it, it was pretty arrogant of me to do that— that's one of the things that God had to work out of me. But I do believe the principle I was fighting for was right."

I agree. So did another pastor I spoke with:

> "At the very beginning," he recalled, "I set boundaries with our congregation. I said, 'Folks, my wife is my *wife*. She's not your *staff member*.'

> "I told them, 'If my wife doesn't want to come to both services, she doesn't have to come to both services. Don't expect her to be involved in every ministry either. If she chooses to, fine. If she doesn't, that's *her* business.'"

Quite a few pastors talked about their families being criticized or scrutinized because of misdirected frustration. One pastor explained his process for handling such situations: "I used to say, 'Look, you want to be mad at me, be mad at me. But don't take it out on my kids.'"

That's excellent fathering—*and* pastoring.

4. Don't bring "church junk" home.

Another way to shield your family is to resist sharing with them all the messy junk that happens in the congregation.

One pastor argued—correctly, I think—that many "pastors create a lot of stress in their families because they go home and they dump all the church stuff on their wife and kids. That's the stupidest thing you can do. God didn't call your wife and kids to pastor the church."

Others reiterated the importance of this:

- "I don't tell my wife half the stuff that happens. I certainly don't tell her about the people who are displeased with me. That's the reason so many pastor's wives are bitter towards the church."

- "You know what's going to upset your wife. You know what she's going to be concerned about. And there's no need in putting her through all that."

- "There are just some things your wife doesn't need to know. She doesn't need to know about every nasty letter or ugly phone call, or every time somebody challenges you about something."

- "I protect my wife from information that I know would cause her to feel stress. I don't go home and talk about this person and this problem 'So-and-so complained to me about this, or somebody's after me about that.'"

My friend, this is wise counsel. Heed it. And if you follow this advice and your spouse acts hurt because "You don't tell me about the details of your day!" and "You don't trust me!" tell her a version of what another pastor shared with me, "My wife respects the fact that, as a pastor, there are just some things that I cannot share with her. The fact is there are some issues, either with people or with situations that just would not be good for her to know because she would take those things to heart."

Another reason not to vent about church problems or badmouth difficult people in the congregation is that it will have unintended consequences on your children. Said one retired pastor: "I didn't talk about church issues at home. My children never heard me criticize the church. I didn't do that. Why? Because even though the people in the church were all imperfect, the church is still the bride of Christ. And we're not to talk negatively about Jesus' bride."

Do you want to protect your family from stress and burnout? Follow the example of this pastor:

> "I made a point to have a normal family life like everybody else. I didn't allow people to hold my kids to a higher standard or to pick on my kids. I never talked negatively about the church or anybody in it in front of them. I never wanted them to hear anything that would cause them to have a negative view of the church."

5. Do everything you can to shield your kids.

In terms of ministry stress on children, the pastors I spoke with were split in their opinions. Ten believed their children did experience stress—ranging from a little to a lot. Nine felt their children were *not* negatively affected by having a father as a pastor.

One of them explained, "My daughter married a pastor, so we must not have messed up too badly. And my son and his wife are actually on staff at their church, so they must not have a bad memory of church being a stressful, unhappy place. For us, that was never a problem."

Another related a different experience: "My second oldest daughter was once not invited to a summer slumber party when she was in the third grade because the girl's parents didn't like me. I found out later she had gone to the little girl and asked, 'Can I come? I'll sleep on the floor.' Just about broke my heart."

Obviously, we can't protect our children from every painful thing in life. But as the shepherds of our homes, we need to be vigilant. It's incumbent upon us to do everything we can to make our kids feel safe.

We talk sometimes about mothers who are like "momma bears" when it comes to protecting their kids. Pastor, your kids need a "poppa bear" too.

6. Make time for your kids.
If you want your kids to have a healthy PK experience, it's not enough to shield them, you also need to spend time with them and pour into them.

Two pastors said their children suffered because pastoral ministry kept them out of the home for large amounts of time. One admitted,

> "I was gone so much in the early years building the church, it definitely hurt my kids. I was away from home almost every night. I joke with people about how my wife read the book *Boundaries* one day and completely messed up *my* life. I didn't have *any* boundaries, really. I was just running and gunning."

> "So, yes, my kids were impacted. I was the absentee father. My thinking was all wrong—I reasoned *Well, they're with me at church events*! But I wasn't giving them enough time at home as 'Dad.'"

There's a haunting scene about that subject in the old Steven Spielberg movie *Hook*. (The movie stars Robin Williams as Peter Pan, all grown up—except that he's become a driven, workaholic corporate takeover artist.)

On what is supposed to be a family vacation, Peter is desperately trying to save a billion-dollar deal. He's in England with his family, but he's not really "there," if you know what I mean. His wife Moira is beyond frustrated, and when he takes yet another call from his partner, Moira angrily grabs his cell phone and hurls it out the window into the snow! Then she makes a speech every dad should hear and heed:

> "Your children love you. They want to play with you! How long do you think that lasts? Soon Jack may not even want you to come to his games. We have a few special years with our

children when they're the ones that want us around. After that, you're going to be running after them for their attention. It's so fast, Peter. It's a few years and then it's OVER. And you are not being careful. And you are missing it!"

Whew! There's some truth for you, straight out of Hollywood. Be careful with that little sliver of time you have with your kids. Don't miss it!

One wise pastor I interviewed noted his habit of regularly scheduled time with his kids: "I budget my time and schedule things proactively. So, when my kids came along this precedent helped me more than anything else. I would proactively schedule nights and reserve time slots for them. That way, when people called and needed something I could legitimately say, 'I'm booked.'"

Make time for your kids. But don't stop there…

7. *Listen* to your kids.

Having kids forces a man to think with a bigger perspective, doesn't it? This bigger perspective can help you handle stress, too. Do you listen to what your children have to say about church?

One pastor said, "I asked my children repeatedly as they were growing up at our church, 'What's it like being the child of a pastor? Is the experience positive, negative, or neutral?' They said, 'We don't even really think of you as the pastor of the church… you are just Dad! It just feels normal.' For me, that was the biggest compliment they could have ever given me."

Dad, limit your schedule for the sake of your kids—and when you're with them, listen! Be present! Turn off your phone! Dare I say it – it is more important for you to be a good father than a good pastor!

8. Don't be a polygamist!

You have a wife (singular). You don't have two wives. You can't be "married" to your sweetheart *and also to your congregation.* That's called "polygamy" (okay, technically, "bigamy"). If you give your congregation the best part of you, your family will suffer—and grow resentful.

One pastor told me: "Looking back on it, I traveled too much. And so my wife had to carry too much of the burden. She never complained, never cried at all. She's always been my biggest supporter. But I put more stress on her than I should have."

Another pastor said he caused stress for his wife by constantly trying to recruit new members and grow his congregation:

> "The first couple of years in the life of our church, I was at somebody's house until about 9 o'clock every night. I would go door to door in neighborhoods. If I saw someone walking, I would walk along with them and talk to them about the Lord. They didn't even have to stop! I was so anxious and eager to talk to anyone about Christ and about how he could impact their life. My wife paid a big price those first couple of years."

Is the ministry hard on families? No doubt. So, please don't make it even harder.

As we've heard here from some experienced pastors, there *are* specific ways you can protect your family.

This is a topic worth deeper reflection...and decisive action.

QUESTIONS FOR REFLECTION / DISCUSSION

- Are you a PK? If so, what was that experience like?
- Can you relate to the pastors who tried to shield their wives from church stress?
- How often does your job have you traveling away from home?
- On average, how many hours are you working each week?
- Do you know firsthand of any pastor's wives or children who are bitter toward the church?

- Do church members treat or view your spouse as your "associate pastor"? How do you respond?

- What's your policy/practice when it comes to sharing "church junk" with your spouse?

- Have you ever shared information with your wife that you wish you hadn't? What happened as a result?

- In what ways has your family been impacted by your stress?

- If your children are grown, are they still involved in the church?

- What would your kids say if they were asked about life as a PK?

- Have your children ever been ostracized or scapegoated for decisions you made or stands you took as a pastor?

CHAPTER 17
Advice for Young Pastors

At the beginning of this book, we met a young pastor named Damian who had sensed the Lord calling him to plant a new church in Los Angeles. Married with two small kids, Damian left a good job in sales with not much more than a vision, a big heart, and some great people skills.

What would our veteran pastors say to a young pastor like Damian? In light of their varied experiences, what advice would they give to *any* young minister? I asked them that question. Here's a summary of what they said.

ACCEPT THE INEVITABILITY OF STRESS

The group was agreed on this point: Stress is going to come your way. Continuously. If it's not one thing, it'll be another. You'll wrestle one difficulty to the ground, get up, catch your breath, turn the corner, and another trial will be waiting for you!

One pastor put it well: "It's not a matter of *if* you're going to avoid stress. You're not. It's a matter of if you're going to overcome it or not, manage it or not, give in to it or not."

This is similar to what Scott Peck said at the start of his bestselling book *The Road Less Traveled*:

"Life is difficult. This is a great truth, one of the greatest truths. It is a great truth because once we truly see this truth, we transcend it. Once we truly know that life is difficult—once we truly understand and accept it—then life is no longer difficult. Because once it is accepted, the fact that life is difficult no longer matters."[29]

Young pastor, there will be challenges in every plan, task, and program you ever attempt. And there will always be strains and pressures in working with staff and volunteers. As pastors we're called to do both—lead *people* in accomplishing the greatest *task* ever given: becoming disciples who make disciples.

We are expected to be pastoral in every situation, whether or not we are "on the clock." That's a stressful job description. The way through all the tension is to ...

CULTIVATE A DEEP RELATIONSHIP WITH JESUS

Here is how another pastor put it:

"Keep yourself alive spiritually. Keep your personal walk with God alive. Because, in truth, we're a lot like a tin can. If we're not careful we can look good on the outside, while being empty inside. That's a can that's easy to crush. When we get like that and the pressure comes, we just collapse. The other, better option is to have internal substance, that internal fullness that enables us to resist the external pressures. In short, keep the can full. Ask Christ to fill you with himself."

Others emphasized this same idea, advising younger pastors to focus most of all on their relationship with God.

BE FAITHFUL TO YOUR CALLING TO PREACH

Several ministers advised younger pastors to concentrate their ministry energy on preaching the Word. One of them explained, "When you preach, you're feeding the flock. Obviously, our first aim is to feed the flock and help them grow in the faith. So do yourself and your church a favor and preach Jesus. Preach the Word of God accurately. Preach it boldly."

That same pastor expressed the need for younger pastors to understand another thing good preaching does:

> "As you faithfully preach the gospel, realize God is using every single sermon, every single week to add another brick to the great building project of creating a gospel-centered culture in your church. So many problems will either be headed off at the pass, or they'll be handled graciously when you have a gospel-driven, Christ-centered, kingdom-focused church culture. So, when you're preaching, you're not just feeding the flock, as important as that is. You're also forming culture."

Preaching brings personal benefits as well. One responded, "I would say to young preachers, preach the Word. If you're preaching the Word effectively that means you're in the Word. And if you're in the Word that means you're growing in the Word. And if you're growing in the Word that means your strength is increasing."

One pastor put it succinctly, "Preach the gospel. Don't get involved in entertainment. Be sure your messages are all about Jesus."

BE A GREAT LOVER OF PEOPLE

The consensus among the pastors I interviewed was that love covers a multitude of pastoral shortcomings and failures. Said one, "Fall in love with those people. Work at genuinely loving those people. Start with the leadership, their wives, and their kids. Learn their names, and just pour yourself into those people. Love them well."

Another said this was his advice to a young or new pastor:

"I would tell him to get a list of all the people in the church. Get a new one every month, if your church is growing. Pray for every person by name, every week. Pray for them whether you like them or not, whether they like you or not. Pray for them. Pray for them. Pray for them.

"I have been doing this now for thirty-eight years. I prayed some out of the church! I had people that were on the fringes, and some of them became my closest friends. But whenever I meet one of these regular church members, I can honestly say, 'I am praying for you and I love you.'"

Other pastors offered assorted "people wisdom" like:

- "The way to overcome challenges and to deal with stress is to value people, build relationships with people, respect people, pour your life into the people, and don't take things personally."

- "I decided to embrace the mindset that it is a privilege to get to serve people and help them with their problems because every one of them is a gem in the making."

- "You have to value people. Many pastors look at people as problems instead of seeing these people as significant. If you don't value people, you will always have problems."

But in all this lavish serving and noble loving, one pastor again warned against trying to do more than is humanly possible:

"I learned through the years that I couldn't visit every home and hold the hand of everyone in the church that had a need. I can't give all my emotional energy to one family because there are others here that also have needs. Remembering this is helpful. It reminds me that I have limitations. Jesus doesn't expect me to crawl up on the cross and die for anyone. He's already done that."

BE WISE ABOUT CHANGING THINGS

Most young pastors show up at a new church with a head full of great ideas and a heart full of big dreams. The tendency is to want to get to work dismantling programs that are outdated and ineffective and start building something new and exciting.

Here's what our wily ministry veterans urged:

"Don't make sudden changes. Just get in there and learn to love people. Build relationships with the people and, once they trust you, they will follow you anywhere."

They urged young ministers to be patient and realistic. It's important to be intentional from the very beginning and to honor the context the church is in.

"I tell guys, when they go to a new church, to just go and listen. If you think you're only going to be there five years, don't change anything. Just love those people. Unless you're going to be there twenty, thirty years, don't you dare go in there and change their governing structure from deacons to elders, or start borrowing money to build buildings! Don't you dare do that, because you will tear the unity of the church apart!

"If you blow up a church like that, then move on to a new church in three or four years, the congregation will be left looking around and thinking, *What did we just do?* and *What do we do now?*

"Don't do it. That's why we have so many unhealthy churches. Not only do pastors not stay very long, but in the brief time they're in a place, they just tinker and experiment. Pastors like that don't have to live with the consequences of their choices. But the people who remain will have to clean up his mess for years to come."

Six pastors said the best advice they could offer to younger pastors is that there will always be problems and stress, but nothing lasts forever.

"Wherever you go… you're going to have problems. You're going to have people that are a headache. And that includes staff because people are just crazy sometimes! It just takes time and patience to build a congregation that will trust you and follow you. You've got to work through the problems." Finally…

CHECK YOUR THOUGHTS.

About situations.

One pastor made this funny admission:

"I have a tendency to get anxious. I even created a word for it… I'm an 'awful-izer.' I imagine the most awful scenarios. Case in point: One night my wife and I are in bed and I hear this tapping sound. And I think to myself, 'Crap, there are squirrels, or mice, or rats in the walls, and they're probably right now chewing through the wiring. I'm probably going to have to get an electrician in here to replace all the wiring in the house. We don't have any savings, and I can't afford that. We're going to end up homeless!'

"It ended up it was just a little bug in a shopping bag."

You'll be less stressed if you learn to take thoughts captive. Don't play the "what if" game. And also be careful when thinking…

About yourself.

Another pastor was blunt about the depression he dealt with as a consequence of stress:

> "In the summer of 1990, I fell into a depression. I got really down on myself. In fact, I actually sat down and I wrote out all the reasons I was no longer qualified to be a pastor. I came up with seven. I remember raising that paper in my office and saying, 'So God, what do you think about *this*?'

> "I hadn't heard from the Lord in a long time, but he spoke to me that day. He said, 'Seven? Is that all you can think of?' Then He was silent for the next few weeks.

> "I believe now that God used that experience and that time in my life to help me understand that he can use me despite my flaws. He also used it to equip me to minister to others who are battling depression. Had I not walked that painful road, I would not have been as sympathetic. I'm convinced God prepares us for future fruitful ministry during the darkest times of our lives."

HANG IN THERE

The consensus among these veteran pastors was that, over time, they *gained new perspectives* and became more *effective at coping* with stress. They learned to *modify* and *adapt* their behaviors. Specifically, they engaged in spiritual disciplines (like prayer, meditation, and worship) and adopted other self-care practices. These practices include delegating and prioritizing responsibilities, seeking social support, taking time off, engaging in regular physical exercise and recreational activities, as well as going on family vacations.

Studies show that roughly one-third of pastors leave the ministry within five years. (How many more at least *contemplate* leaving? It might be close to 100%.)

In my interviews, every single pastor admitted feeling frustrated, excessively stressed, or spiritually stuck at some point in their ministry. And yet they persevered. They hung in there. They learned to eliminate unnecessary stressors. They learned to better cope with unavoidable stressors. Finally, they learned to turn stress into a positive and used it for motivation. Such a journey may be difficult, but it *is* possible.

All the men I spoke with would agree: When we adopt strategies to help us recognize and adapt to occupational stressors, we can stem the tide of pastoral burnout and have long and satisfying careers.

Above all, they would want you to remember that while stress is a fact of life in a fallen world, most specific stressors are short-term. They don't last forever. What's more, the experiences you endure just might serve your ministry in the days to come:

> "Every negative thing that happens in our life, whether it's a stressful marriage or a child that rebels, or whatever it is… opens up a room in your life to host people that are going through the same thing.

> "I was in a group meeting with a large group of people. A man who was not a member of our church was there. I walked up to him because I'd heard that his son had died. I said to him, 'I'm so sorry for what your family is going through right now.' He said, 'Thank you.' Then I said, 'I lost a son too.'

> "When I said that, tears came to his eyes. This big old guy grabbed me and said, 'Nobody understands.' I told him, 'I do. I understand.'

It is true what one theologian has purported, "A thousand sorrows teaches a man to preach."

QUESTIONS FOR REFLECTION / DISCUSSION

- What would you say if you could give advice to your younger minster self?

- What would happen to the current programs at the church you serve if you left tomorrow?

- In what ways has your relationship with God changed throughout your time in ministry?

- What culture has your preaching created in the church where you serve?

- In what ways that you never expected has God used pain in your life to enable you to help others?

CHAPTER 18
Advice for Those Who Are On the Edge

At the beginning of this book, we met three pastors:

- Damian—the dynamic but disorganized rookie pastor of a growing, year-old church plant in Los Angeles

- Brother Charles—the "old-school," 50-something senior pastor of a large, independent megachurch in the Deep South

- Pastor Ken—the weary, spiritually dry 45-year-old pastor of a "stuck" Presbyterian congregation on the east coast

All three are good men. They love God and want to see people come to know Jesus. To piggyback on the title of this book, they each want to have an "enduring ministry."

And yet because of assorted stressors, all three spend at least part of each day "enduring ministry" (pun intended).

What counsel would you offer them? What warnings would you give them about stress and burnout?

Personally, I'd hand them this book and tell them to pay close attention to the wisdom of the older pastors who are quoted extensively in these pages.

When I think about this trio of pastors, there's one I'm really concerned about. Can you guess who it is?

Yep. Pastor Ken. Since we last checked in with him, his serious stress has only intensified. Here's an update.

Three weeks ago, he and his board had a meeting with Ryan (the young, cocky but popular youth pastor). The leadership told Ryan, "Despite your obvious gifting, we no longer believe you're the best fit for this position."

As you might imagine, some in the congregation did not receive this news well. Several families (who have kids in the youth group) have already left the church.

Ken's been to a dozen meetings since the firing. He's gotten six or eight angry emails. The board has been on the receiving end of some harsh criticism.

How has Ken responded to this added stress? He's been going to the office earlier and staying later. Although it's not as if he's being productive. When he's at his desk, he can't seem to focus. He forgets things. He drifts toward mindless tasks, like rearranging his library or cleaning out his old computer files.

Suddenly Ken struggles to make even simple decisions. He puts off returning phone calls. He catches himself daydreaming about being a novelist and living in a remote cabin out west.

Already on the quiet, introverted end of the personality scale, Ken's even more aloof than normal. When he can orchestrate it, he avoids interactions with most church people.

And when he's home? Poor Ken can't fall asleep or stay asleep. He eats nervously and constantly. He's heavier than he's ever been.

This final chapter is a plea to every pastor who is struggling like Ken. If you are just barely hanging on, can I just tell you four true things?

- **Being weary isn't a sin.**

  Feeling tired and empty doesn't mean you're a failure. And it surely doesn't mean God is through with you.

- **What you're experiencing is common.**

  You don't need to feel like a weakling or a freak. Everybody is susceptible. The Bible shows us plenty of leaders who got exhausted serving God. And don't forget. The Almighty knew weariness would be a problem for humanity. That's why he instructed his people to take one day out of seven to stop laboring.

- **There's NO shame in saying, "I'm *not* okay. In fact, I need help!"**

  Isn't this why God sent Jesus…because *nothing* in the world was okay, and *everyone* needed help? Isn't an honest admission like this the first step in experiencing all the goodness the gospel offers? Doesn't the Lord promise to give grace to the humble? Didn't Paul show us that acknowledging our weakness is the prelude for God showing us how strong he is? Finally, can a pastor really be healthy if he goes around pretending he's doing better than he actually is?

- **You don't have to crash and burn. There's another, better option.**

  God can restore you! He can put you on a healthier path. Remember what Isaiah the prophet said? "Though youths grow weary and tired, And vigorous young men stumble badly, Yet those who wait for the Lord *will* gain new strength; They will mount up with wings like eagles, They will run and not get tired, They will walk and not become weary." (Isaiah 40:30–31, NASB95 emphasis added)

THREE SIMPLE STEPS FOR THOSE ON THE EDGE OF BURNOUT

For every guy like Ken, a better ministry experience—and life experience—awaits. But finding it requires you to do three things

1. **Be honest.**

   To come back from the brink of burnout, you've got to be honest with yourself. If you feel overwhelmed, like you're close to losing it, you need to look yourself in the mirror and say, "I can't keep going like this."

   Tell yourself the truth. Then be honest with a few others—your spouse, a trusted friend, a close colleague, your board. (Many of them may be waiting for you to finally admit what they have been seeing for a while!)

2. **Be courageous.**

   With the help of a team of people who (a) understand your struggles; and (b) are *for* you, create a courageous plan for addressing your stress/burnout.

   This plan will necessarily involve an assortment of bold, aggressive actions. It will require making changes—big and small—in your life. For example, you may need to:

   - See a counselor or therapist—and don't be shocked or afraid if they tell you to take an anti-depressant—for a time

   - Explore and address unhealthy, joy-stealing tendencies in your heart like work-a-holism, perfectionism, people-pleasing, trying to control people and outcomes

   - Make radical changes to your schedule and/or job description by making micro changes to your schedule and/or job description.

- Stop being on call 24/7

- Take a class in stress management or setting boundaries or being more assertive

- Let one of your associates handle the preaching for a few months

- Take time off—perhaps even take a sabbatical (For a workaholic like Ken, this will feel like death...even though it is the path to life.)

Steps like these can feel terrifying. That's okay. Courage isn't the absence of fear. It's doing the right things that, for whatever reason, you're afraid to do.

3. **Be patient.**

One pastor—a burnout survivor himself—said:

"I was shocked when my counselor told me, 'You can't rush your recovery, you know. You didn't get to this place of emptiness overnight. So don't expect to get renewed overnight.'

"My first thought was, *That's nuts! I can take a couple weeks off, sleep in, take naps, do some reading, listen to some podcasts, and pray my way out of this.* I discovered I was wrong, and my counselor was right. When I finally got off the church ministry hamster wheel, I felt even *more* tired after a couple weeks of doing nothing! It was weird. It was like my body was letting me know just how spent I really was! I learned that emotional/spiritual weariness is a very different beast than being physically tired."

Once you've been honest with yourself and others...once you've created a courageous plan for getting healthy, then you've got to be patient. Renewal takes time. Finding a saner lifestyle takes time. Regaining your energy takes time.

Could God restore your shriveled-up soul in a heartbeat? Of course! Could he "zap" you with a holy jolt of fresh energy and passion? Sure. Nothing's impossible with God.

More times than not, however, God doesn't seem to be in a hurry. Usually, he uses simple things and small actions. Change usually comes slowly and gradually.

I've noted this previously, but it bears repeating: the pastors I interviewed all developed strong self-care habits that led to a richer experience.

This corresponds with what academics call *altruistic egoism,* which happens to be the optimal approach to managing stress. At the heart of altruistic egoism is self-care. It is the recognition that taking care of my needs enables me to devote energy to other people and other activities. Through self-care, I can enjoy a life full of meaning and purpose, and I can work for the good of others.[30]

Unfortunately, self-care is often mistaken for selfishness—especially among pastors. And it's this misguided interpretation that sets up ministers and other caring professionals for burnout. The pastors I spoke with all recognized that self-care is what enabled them to better serve their congregations.

A common perception among them was that faith in God and a strong sense of calling helped them focus on the big picture, especially when stress was threatening to overwhelm them. And engaging in self-care only served to sharpen and clarify that sense of calling.

As you start to move away from burnout and back toward a place of health, feel free to try new things. Experiment. Say no to more activities… and yes to more rest. Play more. Try to laugh more. Give yourself grace. Abandon things that don't work. Realize it's okay to sit back and just be.

Remember that your worth has zero to do with accomplishments or accolades, ministry failures, or fiascos. You are not loved by God *if* you avoid certain things. Nor are you loved by God *because* you do certain things. You are loved, period. End of story.

Pastor, none of us are truly qualified to do the work of God. Only God can save a soul and change a life. We are simply objects of grace—beloved beggars telling other beggars where they can find treasure. As one pastor expressed it:

> "Spiritually, I had to come to the realization that I'm not the Holy Spirit. I can't force people down the aisle. I have to see myself in proper perspective and not take myself too seriously. I realize I've been called to a position that is far beyond my abilities. That requires me to have a greater dependence on God. It keeps me humble. I think, *I'm just happy to be here!*"

Your current difficulties will get better. Either because they will go, or you will grow. Or both. Longevity and maturity will give you perspective. As one pastor observed:

> "I do think ministry feels less stressful the older I get. If some of the things that happened late in my ministry had happened when I was just starting out, they would have really, really shook me. I guess, just through the experience of dealing with and surviving such things, you begin to process them a little differently. You see them through a different lens. And you see that life goes on. And so you get ready for the next challenge.

> "It's helped me to have some mentors in my life along the way with whom I could share things. They were able to put things into perspective better than I could, helping me see that this is not a life or death situation."

Having an enduring ministry requires enduring ministry—when it gets hard and stressful.

By God's grace, we have everything we need to make it all the way home: The Word of God, the Spirit of God, and the People of God.

Think about what Paul said in his letter to the Church at Corinth:

"For this light momentary affliction is preparing for us an
eternal weight of glory beyond all comparison, as we look not
to the things that are seen but to the things that are unseen.
For the things that are seen are transient, but the
things that are unseen are eternal."
(2 Corinthians 4:17-18 ESV)

"Light momentary affliction"!? This is either the cruelest thing that Paul ever wrote, or one of the most freeing truths about difficulty ever shared.

When we face debilitating diseases, brutal hardships, confusing leadership challenges, and even death itself, we do not think of such things as "light and momentary." But Paul says when our perspective is one of eternity, then we can realize that whatever we face here can never compare to what we get to enjoy forever and ever in the presence of God!

I'll close with the succinct charge given almost 2,000 years ago by the apostle Paul to a young pastor who was facing his share of ministry stressors:

"Fight the good fight of faith" (1 Timothy 6:12, NASB)

In Christ we are more than conquerors.

QUESTIONS FOR REFLECTION / DISCUSSION

- If Pastor Ken were a friend of yours, what would you encourage him to do?

- Why do you think so many stressed-out pastors—who are dangerously close to burnout—are so reluctant to tell themselves or others, "I'm not in a good place. I need help"?

- On a scale of 1-10, with 1 being "My ministry is 100% stress-free" and 10 being "I'm so frazzled, I'm about to do something crazy," where are you on the stress/burnout scale?

- Do you agree that maturity and longevity in ministry give you a better perspective on stress?

- What actual, concrete steps do you need to take to better eliminate or cope with stress?

- What are the best takeaways for you from this book?

RESOURCES

STRESS/BURNOUT SELF-ASSESSMENT
How can I tell when I'm unhealthily stressing out?

☐ Do I look forward to going to work most days?

☐ Am I easily triggered lately? (Do I have an unusually short fuse?)

☐ Is it hard for me to relax and "go off duty"?

☐ Do I feel out of control much of the time?

☐ Do I find I am becoming more of a "control freak"?

☐ Do I have a hard time focusing?

☐ Do I feel run-down and weary a lot?

☐ Does my dentist tell I am grinding my teeth?

☐ Does my doctor tell me my blood pressure is high?

☐ Have I noticed a change in my sleep habits? (e.g., sleeping longer than normal, insomnia, waking up early, etc.)

☐ Am I gaining weight (or losing weight)?

☐ Do I have low libido or an inability to perform in the bedroom?

☐ Do I get frequent headaches?

☐ Have I become unusually moody?

☐ Do I feel depressed (down on myself or hopeless about life)?

☐ Am I procrastinating more than normal?

☐ Do I find I put off making decisions?

☐ Do I have a hard time turning off my brain?

☐ Am I forgetting things more than normal?

☐ Is my stomach acting up (i.e., diarrhea, constipation, queasy feelings)?

☐ Do I catch myself biting my nails or fidgeting or pacing excessively?

☐ Do I feel especially restless?

☐ Am I nervous or anxious much of the time?

☐ Do I find I want to avoid people—not just certain people, but people in general?

☐ Am I unusually pessimistic or gloomy?

☐ Am I craving food all the time (or find I'm disinterested in eating)?

☐ Does my heart race at times—or do I get chest pains?

☐ Do I daydream frequently about escaping?

☐ Am I losing the capacity to care?

☐ Do I feel like I'm just going through the motions?

☐ Am I giving in easily to temptation?

☐ Do I find myself pulling away from people?

☐ Does denominational red tape ever keep me from living out my calling?

☐ Do I feel supported by staff members and board members?

☐ Am I starting to complain a lot?

☐ Have I forgotten how to laugh and have fun?

☐ Do I get especially defensive in the face of criticism?

☐ Am I being passive-aggressive towards people who annoy me?

☐ Do I often feel "in over my head" because I haven't been trained in certain aspects of organization management (e.g., conflict resolution, collaborative decision-making, program development, and agenda-setting)?

REMEMBERING WHAT'S TRUE:
Hard Truths We Need to Internalize

- Self-care is not selfishness.

- The church you serve does not *need* you to be available 24/7 to survive.

- Stress is inevitable.

- Perfectionism is a bad thing and a futile goal. (There is no greater frustration than being an imperfect perfectionist.)

- "Success" in ministry + failure at home = failure

- Though stress will never completely go away, some stressors are only for a season.

- Far better to wear out gradually, than to flame out in a scandalous way.

- You have all the time you need to do all the things God has called you to do.

- God *will* give you more than you can handle…so you will turn to Him and cast your cares on Him. *With Him*, there is nothing you can't handle.

- You can transform some stress into motivation.

ABOUT THE AUTHOR:

Jackson Andrew Hester is the lead pastor of Mars Hill Church with campuses in Mobile and Fairhope Alabama. He also is an adjunct professor at the University of Mobile in Mobile, Alabama. He holds a BA in Communication from that university, a MDiv from Southwestern Seminary in Fort Worth, Texas, as well as a Doctor of Educational Ministry and a PhD from Southern Seminary in Louisville, Kentucky. Jackson has served churches in Texas and Alabama and was the founding pastor of Mars Hill where he has served for 18 years now.

Jackson is married to Brandi Hester and they have three children, Collin, Caleb, and Caroline.

RECOMMENDATIONS:

As the church works to push back lostness throughout North America, pastors are the point of the spear. They are critical to our work in fulfilling the mission of God in our communities. Today too many are stressed out, worn out and burnt out. The last two years have been unbelievably tough on pastors. Jackson Hester's new book, Enduring Ministry, *is like a lifeline to these wounded heroes who are on the frontlines of ministry. By leveraging the wisdom of pastors with years of ministry experience, Jackson has given a gift to the church—one that I believe can help save the ministries of many worn out pastors.*

Kevin Ezell
President
North American Mission Board, SBC

Though written for pastors, Enduring Ministry: Wisdom from Veteran Pastors for Managing Stress & Avoiding Burnout is a tremendous resource for leaders in every profession. Whether it is the workplace, health issues, or family challenges, this book provides real-life examples and practical advice on how to tackle the stress and potential burnout that all leaders face. No matter your profession, you will be challenged and encouraged by this book.

John Smith
Interim President
University of South Alabama

"Every minister faces many challenges to his ministry. Burnout is the unwanted result of stress that is not healthy. Remember that any deadline is stress! Everyone of us faces deadlines every week. In addition to the many natural

stressors in ministry in helping people in their spiritual journey, every dead-line is stress. This book will increase your ability to recognize and manage the stress you face. It will lighten your way each step of the way."

Jimmy Draper
President Emeritus LifeWay

END NOTES

1   LifeWay Research, "Reasons for Attrition among Pastors," accessed on
    September 1, 2017;
    LifeWayresearch.com/2015/09/01/despite-stressors-few-pastors-give-up-on-
    ministry, 10.

2   Charlton et al., "Clergy Work-Related Psychological Health," 133.

3   Christina Maslach, Wilmar B. Schaufeli, and Michael P. Leiter, "Job Burnout,"
    Annual Review of Psychology 52.1 (2001): 397.

4   Rae Jean Proeschold-Bell and Sara LeGrand, "Physical Health Functioning
    among United Methodist Clergy," Journal of Religious Health 51 (2012):
    734-42.

5   Andrew Weaver and Kevin Flannelly, "Mental Health Issues among Clergy
    and Other Religious Professionals: A Review of Research," Journal of
    Pastoral Care & Counseling 56 (2002): 393-403.

6   Angela Duckworth, Grit: The Power of Passion and Perseverance (New York:
    Simon and Schuster, 2016), 50.

7   Rodger Charlton et al., "Clergy Work-Related Psychological Health:
    Listening to the Ministers of Word and Sacrament within the United
    Reformed Church in England," Pastoral Psychology 58.2 (2009): 133.

8   See Laura K. Barnard and John F. Curry, "The Relationship of Clergy
    Burnout to Self-Compassion and Other Personality Dimensions," Pastoral
    Psychology 61. 2 (2012): 149-63.

9   Michael Jenkins and Keith Wulff, "Austin Presbyterian Theological
    Seminary's Clergy Burnout Survey," Congregations 5 (2002), accessed July
    17, 2013, http://oldsite.alban.org/uploadedFiles/.
    Alban/Conversation/pdf/AustinGrad2-app.pdf. See also Daniel Spaite, Time
    Bomb in the Church (Kansas City, MO: Beacon Hill, 1999).

10 See Kathleen Galek et al., "Burnout, Secondary Traumatic Stress, and Social
    Support," Pastoral Psychology 60.5 (2011): 635.

11 Charles Figley, "Compassion Fatigue: Toward a New Understanding of
    the Costs of Caring," in Secondary Traumatic Stress: Self-Care Issues for
    Clinicians, Researchers, and Educators, ed. Beth H. Stamm (Lutherville,
    MD: Sidran, 1995), 3-28; Chenelle Buys and Sebastian Rothmann, "Burnout
    and Engagement of Reformed Church Ministers," SA Journal of Industrial
    Psychology 36.1 (2010): 1; Stephen M. Beaumont, "Pastoral Counseling

Down Under: A Survey of Australian Clergy," Pastoral Psychology 60.1 (2011): 117; Jill Anne Hendron, Pauline Irving, and Brian Taylor, "The Unseen Cost: A Discussion of the Secondary Traumatization Experience of the Clergy," Pastoral Psychology 61.2 (2012): 221; Gail Kinman, Obrene McFall, and Joanna Rodriguez, "The Cost of Caring? Emotional Labour, Wellbeing and the Clergy," Pastoral Psychology 60.5 (2011): 671.

12   Louis J. Spencer, Bruce E. Winston, and Mihai C. Bocarnea, "Validating a Practitioner's Instrument Measuring the Level of Pastors' Risk of Termination/Exit from the Church: Discovering Vision Conflict and Compassion Fatigue as Key Factors," Pastoral Psychology 61 (2012): 85, 87, 91.

13   Bob Burns, Tasha D. Chapman, and Donald C. Guthrie, Resilient Ministry: What Pastors Told Us About Surviving and Thriving (Downers Grove, IL: IVP, 2013), 199-200.

14   J.M. Faucett, R.F. Corwyn, and T.H. Poling, "Clergy Role Stress: Interactive Effects of Role Ambiguity and Role Conflict on Intrinsic Job Satisfaction," Pastoral Psychology 62 (2013): 291-304; Garner, "Interpersonal Criticism and the Clergy," 2.

15   Randall, "Examining Thoughts," 186-87; Wells, "The Effects of Work-Related and Boundary-Related Stress," 101; Wells, "The Moderating Effects," 873.

16   Marcus N. Tanner and Anisa M. Zvonkovic, "Forced to Leave: Forced Termination Experiences of Assemblies of God Clergy and Its Connection to Stress and Well-Being Outcomes," Pastoral Psychology 60.5 (2011): 713; Marcus N. Tanner, Jeffrey N. Wherry, and Anisa M. Zvonkovic, "Clergy Who Experience Trauma as a Result of Forced Termination," Journal of Religion and Health 52.4 (2013): 1281.

17   Randy Garner, "Interpersonal Criticism and the Clergy," Journal of Pastoral Care and Counseling 67.1 (2013): 2, 5-6.

18   Sonnentag, Kuttler, and Fritz, "Job Stressors, Emotional Exhaustion, and Need for Recovery," 355; Burns, Chapman, and Guthrie, Resilient Ministry, 178.

19   Benjamin R. Doolittle, "The Impact of Behaviors upon Burnout among Parish-Based Clergy," Journal of Religion and Health 49.1 (2010): 90-91, 93.

20   Doolittle, "The Impact of Behaviors," 93; Scott and Lovell, "The Rural Pastors Initiative," 93; Sabine Sonnentag, Iris Kuttler, and Charlotte Fritz,

"Job Stressors, Emotional Exhaustion, and Need for Recovery: A Multi-Source Study on the Benefits of Psychological Detachment," Journal of Vocational Behavior 76.3 (2010): 355.

21 Ryan C. Staley, Mark R. McMinn, Kathleen Gathercoal, and Kurt Free, "Strategies Employed by Clergy to Prevent and Cope with Interpersonal Isolation," Pastoral Psychology 62.6 (2013): 843.

22 Kelvin Randall, "Examining Thoughts about Leaving the Ministry among Anglican Clergy in England and Wales: Demographic, Churchmanship, Personality, and Work-Related Psychological Health Factors," Practical Theology 6 (2013): 186-87; Carl R. Wells, "The Moderating Effects of Congregational and Denominational Support on the Impact of Stress on Clerical Emotional and Physical Health Status," Pastoral Psychology 62.6 (2013): 873.

23 Greg Scott and Rachel Lovell, "The Rural Pastors Initiative: Addressing Isolation and Burnout in Rural Ministry," Pastoral Psychology 64.1 (2015): 71.

24 Leslie J. Francis et al., "Work-Related Psychological Health among Clergy Serving in the Presbyterian Church (USA): Testing the Idea of Balanced Affect," Review of Religious Research 53.1 (2011): 16.

25 George Barna, "Report Examines the State of Mainline Protestant Churches," accessed November 11, 2016, https://www.barna.com/research/report-examines-the-state-of-mainline-protestant-churches/#.

26 Diane Chandler, "Pastoral Burnout and the Impact of Personal Spiritual Renewal, Rest-Taking, and Support System Practices," Pastoral Psychology 58 (2009): 283, 285.

27 Galek et al., "Burnout, Secondary Traumatic Stress, and Social Support," 635.

28 Siang-Yang Tan and Melissa Castillo, "Self-Care and Beyond: A Brief Literature Review from a Christian Perspective," Journal of Psychology and Christianity 33.1 (2014): 3.

29 M. Scott Peck, The Road Less Traveled (New York: Touchstone, 1978), 15.

30 Hans Selye, "Forty Years of Stress Research: Principal Remaining Problems and Misconceptions," Canadian Medical Association Journal 115.1 (1976): 53.